NATIONAL GEOGRAPHIC Atlas of t

WORLD

for Intermediate Students

Mc Graw Hill **Macmillan McGraw-Hill**

New York   Farmington

In This Atlas...

Introduction to the World

North America

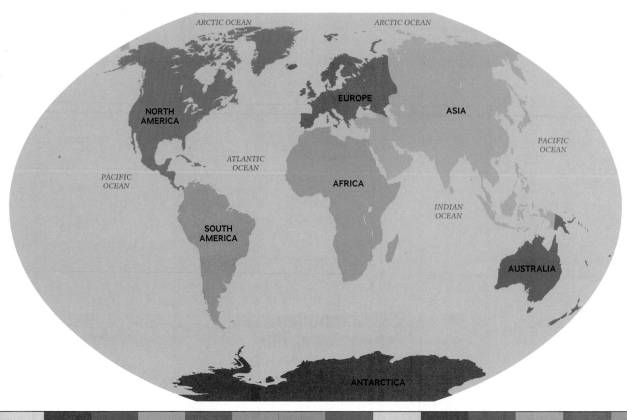

South America

Asia

Africa

Australia & Oceania

Europe

Antarctica

The World

ENVIRONMENTS

Earth's surface is divided between areas of land and water. The land areas, called continents, are made up of many different environments. Near the equator tropical forests are home to plants and animals that thrive in the warm, humid climate. Other environments include rugged mountains and dry deserts. Different kinds of plants and animals have adapted to these environments. Most people live on gently rolling plains.

▼ *Mountain chains and volcanic islands rise up from the ocean depths. Warm and cold currents flow through the oceans, creating habitats for many different types of sea life.*

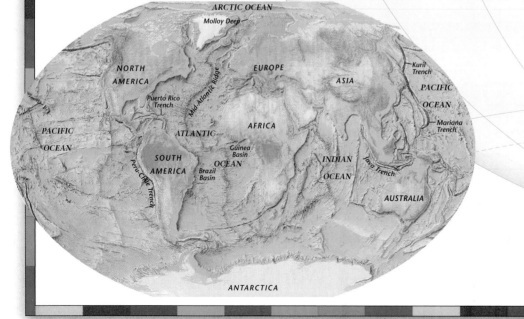

Map labels:

Queen Elizabeth Islands, Ellesmere Island, Chukchi Sea, SIBERIA, Beaufort Sea, Brooks Range, Yukon, Victoria Island, Baffin Bay, Baffin Island, Bering Sea, Mackenzie, Great Bear Lake, Coast Mountains, Mt. McKinley 20,320 ft (6,194 m), NORTH AMERICA, Canadian, Great Slave Lake, Hudson Bay, Labrador Sea, Labrador, Aleutian Islands, Vancouver Island, Cascade Range, Nelson, Lake Winnipeg, Great Plains, Great Lakes, Canadian Shield, Island of Newfoundland, Great Salt Lake, Missouri, Central Lowland, Appalachian Mountains, Death Valley -282 ft (-86 m), Colorado, Rio Grande, Sierra Madre Oriental, TROPIC OF CANCER, Baja California, Sierra Madre Occidental, Gulf of Mexico, West Indies, Greater Antilles, CENTRAL AMERICA, Caribbean Sea, Lesser Antilles, ATLANTIC, POLYNESIA, Hawaiian Islands, PACIFIC, Line Islands, OCEAN, 150°W, 120°W, EQUATOR, 90°W, Galápagos Islands, Llanos, Orinoco, Guiana Highlands, Negro, Amazon, Amazon, Marquesas Islands, Basin, SOUTH, Madeira, Tocantins, Samoa Is., Tuamotu Archipelago, Cook Islands, Society Is., Tahiti, Mato Grosso Plateau, Brazilian Highlands, São Francisco, Tonga Is., Fiji Is., Lake Titicaca, ANDES, AMERICA, Austral Islands, TROPIC OF CAPRICORN, Easter Island, Gran Chaco, Paraguay, Paraná, 30°S, Cerro Aconcagua 22,834 ft (6,960 m), Pampas, Isla Grande de Chiloé, Valdés Peninsula -131 ft (-40 m), Patagonia, Falkland Islands, Strait of Magellan, Tierra del Fuego, South Shetland Islands, Antarctic Peninsula, Bellingshausen Sea, Ellsworth Land, Marie Byrd Land, Vinson Massif 16,067 ft (4,897 m), TRANSANTARCTIC

ARCTIC OCEAN, Molloy Deep, NORTH AMERICA, EUROPE, ASIA, Kuril Trench, PACIFIC OCEAN, Mid-Atlantic Ridge, Puerto Rico Trench, ATLANTIC, AFRICA, Guinea Basin, Mariana Trench, PACIFIC OCEAN, SOUTH AMERICA, OCEAN, Brazil Basin, INDIAN OCEAN, Java Trench, Peru-Chile Trench, AUSTRALIA, ANTARCTICA

ARCTIC OCEAN

Greenland
Sea

Svalbard
Novaya Zemlya
Kara
Sea
Laptev Sea
East Siberian Sea

ENLAND

ARCTIC CIRCLE

Norwegian Sea
Barents Sea

eland

British
Isles
Great
Britain
North
Sea
Baltic Sea
Scandinavia
Ural Mountains
Ob
West
Siberian
Plain
Irtysh
Central
Siberian
Plateau
Lena
Angara
Lena
60°N
Bering Sea
Kamchatka
Peninsula
Sea of
Okhotsk
Aleutian Is.

Ireland

EUROPE
Alps
Danube
Northern European Plain
Volga
El'brus
18,510 ft
(5,642 m)
The Steppes
Aral
Sea
Ob
S I B E R I A
Altay Mountains
Lake
Baikal
Amur
Hokkaido
JAPAN
Kuril Islands
Honshu

res
Mediterranean Sea
Black Sea
Caucasus Mts.
Caspian Sea
Tian Shan
ASIA
Taklimakan
Desert
Kunlun Mountains
GOBI
North China Plain
Yellow (Huang)
Sea of
Japan
Korea
30°N
Nampo Shoto

ary
ds

Atlas Mountains
Dead Sea
-1,349 ft
(-411 m)
Zagros Mountains
Plateau of Tibet
Yellow
Sea
Yangtze
(Chang)
East
China
Sea
Ryukyu Islands

de
ds

SAHARA
Libyan Desert
Nile
ARABIAN
PENINSULA
Persian Gulf
HIMALAYA
Brahmaputra
Mt. Everest
29,035 ft
(8,850 m)
Ganges
Salween
Taiwan
PACIFIC

S A H E L
AFRICA
Niger
White Nile
Blue Nile
Red Sea
Gulf of Aden
Ethiopian
Highlands
Somali
Peninsula
INDIA
Deccan
Plateau
Bay of
Bengal
Andaman Sea
Mekong
Indochina
Peninsula
Hainan
South
China
Sea
Luzon
Philippine
Sea
Mariana
Islands
OCEAN

Upper Guinea

Arabian
Sea
Andaman
Islands
Sri Lanka
Nicobar Is.
Philippine Islands
MICRONESIA
Marshall
Islands

Gulf of Guinea
Congo
Lake
Victoria
Great Rift Valley
Kilimanjaro
19,340 ft
(5,895 m)
Maldive
Islands
60°E
90°E
Malay
Peninsula
Borneo
INDONESIA
Greater Sunda
Islands
Moluccas
Celebes
New
Guinea
150°E
EQUATOR
0°
Gilbert
Islands
MELANESIA
Bismarck
Archipelago

OCEAN
Lower Guinea
Congo
Basin
Lake
Tanganyika
Seychelles
INDIAN
Sumatra
Java
Arafura
Sea
Solomon
Islands

Zambezi
Madagascar
OCEAN
Coral
Sea
Vanuatu
Fiji
Islands

Namib Desert
Kalahari
Desert
Drakensberg
Mascarene Islands
Great
Sandy Desert
Great Dividing Range
New
Caledonia

AUSTRALIA
Lake Eyre
-52 ft, (-16 m)
Great
Victoria Desert
Central Lowlands
Tasman
Sea
30°S

0   miles   2000
0 kilometers 3000

Winkel Tripel Projection
Kerguélen Islands
Darling
Murray
Mt. Kosciuszko
7,310 ft
(2,228 m)
NEW
ZEALAND
North
Island
South
Island

South
Sandwich
Islands
Tasmania

ANTARCTIC CIRCLE
Auckland
Islands
60°S

Queen Maud Land

OUNTAINS
ANTARCTICA
Transantarctic Mountains
Victoria Land

The World

People have divided Earth's land area into political units called countries. The lines that mark these political divisions are called boundaries. At the start of the 21st century, there were 191 independent countries. Some, such as Russia and Canada, cover large expanses of land. Others, such as Kuwait and Rwanda, are small in area.

People across continents and countries have a variety of different cultures. A country's culture includes languages, religions, foods, sports, celebrations and many other ways of living. Find out more about one of the countries on the map. What is one way its culture is like the culture of the United States? What is one way that its culture is different?

▶ *Near the North and South Poles, Earth's extremes do not have countries, boundaries, or permanent populations. The cold waters of the Arctic Ocean surround the North Pole. The frozen ice fields of Antarctica surround the South Pole.*

Chukchi Sea
RUSSIA
Bering Sea
Alaska (U.S.)
60°N
Aleutian Islands
Gulf of Alaska
Beaufort Sea
Banks Island
Victoria Island
Great Bear Lake
Great Slave Lake
Queen Elizabeth Islands
Ellesmere Island
Baffin Island
Baffin Bay

CANADA
Hudson Bay
Lake Winnipeg
Great Lakes
Ottawa
Labrador Sea
Island of Newfoundland

30°N
UNITED STATES
Great Salt Lake
Los Angeles
New York
Washington, D.C.

MEXICO
Gulf of Mexico
México
Havana
Nassau
BAHAMAS
CUBA
BELIZE
Belmopan
GUATEMALA
Guatemala
San Salvador
EL SALVADOR
HONDURAS
Tegucigalpa
NICARAGUA
Managua
COSTA RICA
San José
Panama
PANAMA
Kingston
JAMAICA
HAITI
Port-au-Prince
DOMINICAN REP.
Santo Domingo
Puerto Rico (U.S.)
Virgin Is. (U.S. & U.K.)
ST. KITTS & NEVIS
ANTIGUA & BARBUDA
Guadeloupe (France)
DOMINICA
Martinique (France)
ST. LUCIA
BARBADOS
ST. VINCENT & THE GRENADINES
GRENADA
TRINIDAD AND TOBAGO

TROPIC OF CANCER

Hawaiian Islands (U.S.)

PACIFIC

Kiritimati

KIRIBATI

150°W   120°W   EQUATOR   90°W

0°

OCEAN

Marquesas Islands (France)

SAMOA
Apia
American Samoa (U.S.)

French Polynesia (France)

TONGA
Nuku'alofa

TROPIC OF CAPRICORN

Chatham Is. (N.Z.)

Caribbean Sea

ATLANTI

VENEZUELA
Caracas
Georgetown
Paramaribo
French Guiana (France)
SURINAME
GUYANA
COLOMBIA
Bogotá
Quito
ECUADOR
Galápagos Islands (Ecuador)
PERU
Lima
La Paz
BOLIVIA
Sucre
PARAGUAY
Asunción

BRAZIL
Brasília
São Paulo
Rio de Janeiro

30°S
Santiago
CHILE
Buenos Aires
URUGUAY
Montevideo
ARGENTINA

Falkland Islands (U.K.)
Tierra del Fuego
Strait of Magellan
Drake Passage

60°S

Ross Sea

| 0 | miles | 2000 |
| 0 | kilometers | 3000 |

Winkel Tripel Projection

Alaska (U.S.)
0   mi   600
0   km   900
Azimuthal Equidistant Projection
180°
150°W   150°E
East Siberian Sea
New Siberian Islands
Laptev Sea
75°N
Beaufort Sea
Banks Island
Victoria Island
CANADA
Ellesmere Island
Baffin Island
Baffin Bay
90°W
ARCTIC
North Pole
OCEAN
RUSSIA
Franz Josef Land
Novaya Zemlya
60°E
Kara Sea
Barents Sea
Svalbard (Norway)
30°E
Greenland (Denmark)
60°W
Norwegian Sea
ARCTIC CIRCLE
30°W
ICELAND
NORWAY
SWEDEN
FINLAND

ARCTIC OCEAN

Franz Josef Land
Severnaya Zemlya
New Siberian Islands
East Siberian Sea

Greenland (Denmark)
Greenland Sea
Svalbard (Norway)
Barents Sea
Novaya Zemlya
Kara Sea
Laptev Sea

ARCTIC CIRCLE
Norwegian Sea
60°N
Bering Sea

ICELAND
Reykjavík
NORWAY
SWEDEN
FINLAND
Oslo
Stockholm
Helsinki
North Sea
EST.
LATV.
LITH.
Minsk
Moscow

R U S S I A

Sea of Okhotsk
Kamchatka Peninsula
Sakhalin

UNITED KINGDOM
DENMARK
Copenhagen
Berlin
POLAND
BELARUS
UKRAINE
Astana
KAZAKHSTAN
Aral Sea
Ulaanbaatar
MONGOLIA
Hokkaido

IRELAND
Dublin
London
NETH.
BELG.
GERMANY
CZECH REP.
AUSTRIA
HUNG.
SLOVAKIA
MOLD.
ROMANIA
Kiev
Warsaw
UZBEKISTAN
Tashkent
Bishkek
KYRGYZSTAN
NORTH KOREA
Pyongyang
Seoul
JAPAN
Honshu
Tokyo

Paris
FRANCE
SWITZ.
SLOV.
CRO.
ITALY
Rome
BULGARIA
Black Sea
GEORGIA
ARM.
AZERB.
TURKMENISTAN
Ashgabat
Dushanbe
TAJIKISTAN
Beijing
C H I N A
SOUTH KOREA
Osaka
Kyushu
30°N

PORTUGAL
Lisbon
SPAIN
Madrid
ALBANIA
MACED.
GREECE
Athens
Ankara
TURKEY
CYPRUS
LEBANON
ISRAEL
SYRIA
IRAQ
Baghdad
Tehran
IRAN
AFGHANISTAN
Kabul
Islamabad
Shangahai

The People's Republic of China claims Taiwan as its 23rd province.

TAIWAN
Taipei
PACIFIC

Azores (Portugal)
Madeira Is. (Portugal)
MOROCCO
Rabat
Algiers
TUNISIA
Tunis
Tripoli
Mediterranean Sea
Cairo
JORDAN
KUWAIT
BAHRAIN
QATAR
U.A.E.
Riyadh
SAUDI ARABIA
New Delhi
NEPAL
Kathmandu
Thimphu
BHUTAN
BANGLADESH
Dhaka
MYANMAR (BURMA)
Hanoi
Hainan
Philippine Sea
Northern Mariana Islands (U.S.)
OCEAN

Canary Is. (Spain)
Western Sahara (Morocco)
ALGERIA
LIBYA
EGYPT
Red Sea
Khartoum
ERITREA
Asmara
YEMEN
Sanaa
Arabian Sea
Karachi
PAKISTAN
Mumbai (Bombay)
INDIA
Calcutta
Bay of Bengal
Yangon
Vientiane
LAOS
VIETNAM
THAILAND
Bangkok
Luzon
Manila
PHILIPPINES
MARSHALL ISLANDS

MAURITANIA
Nouakchott
CAPE VERDE
GAMBIA
SENEGAL
MALI
NIGER
Niamey
CHAD
N'Djamena
SUDAN
OMAN
Muscat
DJIBOUTI
Addis Ababa
Socotra (Yemen)
SRI LANKA
Colombo
Sri Jayewardenepura Kotte
Male
MALDIVES
60°E
90°E
CAMBODIA
Phnom Penh
Mindanao
PALAU
FEDERATED STATES OF MICRONESIA
150°E
EQUATOR
0°
KIRIBATI

GUINEA-BISSAU
Bissau
GUINEA
Conakry
SIERRA LEONE
Freetown
LIBERIA
Monrovia
BURKINA FASO
Ouagadougou
BENIN
NIGERIA
Abuja
Lagos
CENTRAL AFRICAN REPUBLIC
Bangui
ETHIOPIA
SOMALIA
Mogadishu
BRUNEI
Bandar Seri Begawan
Kuala Lumpur
MALAYSIA
SINGAPORE
NAURU

Yamoussoukro
CÔTE D'IVOIRE
GHANA
Accra
TOGO
Lomé
Porto Novo
CAMEROON
Yaoundé
EQ. GUINEA
Libreville
GABON
CONGO
Brazzaville
DEMOCRATIC REPUBLIC OF THE CONGO
UGANDA
Kampala
RWANDA
Kigali
BURUNDI
Bujumbura
KENYA
Nairobi
Dar es Salaam
Borneo
Celebes
INDONESIA
Jakarta
Java
New Guinea
PAPUA NEW GUINEA
Port Moresby
SOLOMON ISLANDS
Honiara
TUVALU

SAO TOME AND PRINCIPE
CABINDA (Angola)
Kinshasa
TANZANIA
SEYCHELLES
INDIAN
East Timor
Coral Sea

Luanda
ANGOLA
Lilongwe
MALAWI
ZAMBIA
Lusaka
MOZAMBIQUE
COMOROS
Moroni
Antananarivo
MAURITIUS
Port Louis
OCEAN
Réunion (France)
New Caledonia (France)
VANUATU
Port-Vila
FIJI
Suva

NAMIBIA
Windhoek
BOTSWANA
Gabbrone
ZIMBABWE
Harare
Pretoria
MADAGASCAR
AUSTRALIA
30°S

Bloemfontein
SWAZILAND
Maputo
SOUTH AFRICA
LESOTHO
Great Australian Bight
Canberra
Tasman Sea
North Island

Cape Town
Kerguélen Islands (France)
Tasmania
NEW ZEALAND
Wellington
South Island

ANTARCTIC CIRCLE

A N T A R C T I C A

ATLANTIC OCEAN
ANTARCTIC CIRCLE
Weddell Sea
Antarctic Peninsula
75°S
60°E
INDIAN OCEAN
Ronne Ice Shelf
ANTARCTICA
90°W
West Antarctica
South Pole
East Antarctica
90°E
Ross Ice Shelf
Ross Sea
PACIFIC OCEAN
30°W
120°E
0 mi 600
0 km 900
Azimuthal Equidistant Projection
180°

World Information

▶ **Earth's Land & Water**

Earth is sometimes called the "water planet" because 71% of its surface is covered by water. Only 29% is covered by land.

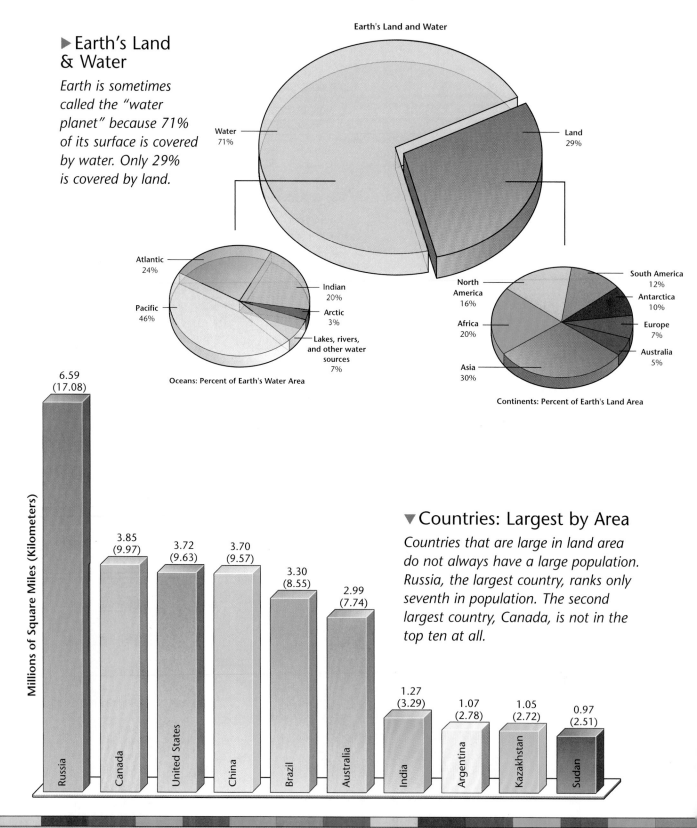

Earth's Land and Water

Water 71%

Land 29%

Oceans: Percent of Earth's Water Area

Atlantic 24%

Pacific 46%

Indian 20%

Arctic 3%

Lakes, rivers, and other water sources 7%

Continents: Percent of Earth's Land Area

North America 16%

South America 12%

Antarctica 10%

Europe 7%

Australia 5%

Asia 30%

Africa 20%

▼ **Countries: Largest by Area**

Countries that are large in land area do not always have a large population. Russia, the largest country, ranks only seventh in population. The second largest country, Canada, is not in the top ten at all.

Millions of Square Miles (Kilometers)

- Russia: 6.59 (17.08)
- Canada: 3.85 (9.97)
- United States: 3.72 (9.63)
- China: 3.70 (9.57)
- Brazil: 3.30 (8.55)
- Australia: 2.99 (7.74)
- India: 1.27 (3.29)
- Argentina: 1.07 (2.78)
- Kazakhstan: 1.05 (2.72)
- Sudan: 0.97 (2.51)

Millions of People

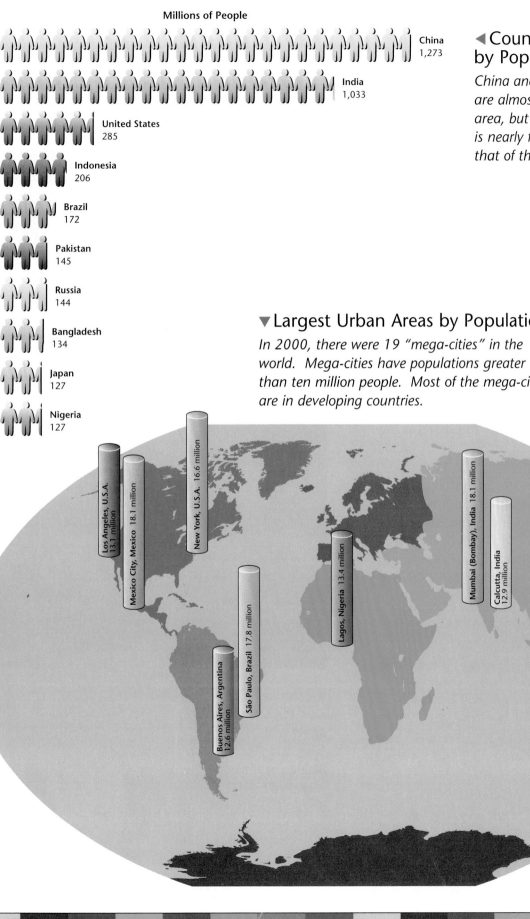

China 1,273

India 1,033

United States 285

Indonesia 206

Brazil 172

Pakistan 145

Russia 144

Bangladesh 134

Japan 127

Nigeria 127

◄ Countries: Largest by Population

China and the United States are almost the same size in area, but China's population is nearly five times larger than that of the U.S.

▼ Largest Urban Areas by Population

In 2000, there were 19 "mega-cities" in the world. Mega-cities have populations greater than ten million people. Most of the mega-cities are in developing countries.

Los Angeles, U.S.A. 13.1 million

Mexico City, Mexico 18.1 million

New York, U.S.A. 16.6 million

Buenos Aires, Argentina 12.6 million

São Paulo, Brazil 17.8 million

Lagos, Nigeria 13.4 million

Mumbai (Bombay), India 18.1 million

Calcutta, India 12.9 million

Shanghai, China 12.9 million

Tokyo, Japan 26.4 million

North America

North America is a continent of contrasts: tall snow-capped mountains, deep, winding canyons, steamy tropical forests. Canada is the second largest country in the world, but the United States has about ten times more people than Canada. The largest city is Mexico City, Mexico.

Many people live on farms that produce food that is traded around the world. Most North Americans, however, live in cities where they work in industries and services. Most people speak Spanish or English, but some speak French or native languages.

Immigration into the United States

People moving from other countries have increased the population of the United States. In the past most immigrants have come from Europe. Today most come from Asia and Latin America. This graph shows the ten largest groups coming to the U.S. in 1998.

Number of Immigrants (1998)

Country	Number
Mexico	131,575
China	36,884
India	36,482
Philippines	34,466
Dominican Republic	20,387
Vietnam	17,649
Cuba	17,375
Jamaica	15,146
El Salvador	14,590
Korea	14,268

▶ *Polar bears, with their thick layers of fur, have adapted to life on the frozen shores of the Arctic Ocean.*

Arctic Canada

U.S.A.

◀ *Over thousands of years the waters of the Colorado River have cut down through rock to create the Grand Canyon in Arizona. The rock layers visible in the canyon walls tell a story of Earth's geologic past.*

Mexico

▲ *Religious festivals such as this one in Puebla often combine Spanish traditions and native legends.*

Canada

▲ *Vancouver's modern skyline rises up on Canada's west coast. This city is a gateway for trade and immigration from the Pacific region.*

ASIA

North Pole

EUROPE

Arctic Ocean

Chukchi Sea

Bering Sea

Aleutian Islands

Queen Elizabeth Islands

Ellesmere Island

ARCTIC CIRCLE

0°

Greenland

Beaufort Sea

Baffin Bay

20°W

Brooks Range

Mt. McKinley 20,320 ft (6,194 m) ▲ Highest point in North America

Yukon

Victoria Island

Baffin Island

Kodiak I. Mt. Logan 19,550 ft (5,959 m) +

Mackenzie

Great Bear Lake

Great Slave Lake

Labrador Sea

Labrador

Island of Newfoundland

40°W

Gulf of Alaska

Peace

Hudson Bay

160°W

40°N

Queen Charlotte Islands

Coast Mountains

Churchill

Saskatchewan

CANADIAN SHIELD

Vancouver Island

Columbia

Lake Winnipeg

Great Lakes

St. Lawrence

Nova Scotia

Atlantic Ocean

Cascade Range

Snake

ROCKY MOUNTAINS

Great Plains

Missouri

Mississippi

Death Valley -282 ft (-86 m) ▼ Lowest point in North America

Great Salt Lake

Central Lowland

Ohio

Appalachian Mts.

Bermuda Islands

Colorado

Arkansas

COASTAL PLAINS

Mississippi

Sierra Madre Occidental

Sierra Madre Oriental

TROPIC OF CANCER

20°N

Baja California

Lake Okeechobee

20°N

Gulf of Mexico

Bahama Islands

West Indies

140°W

Rio Grande

Cuba

Hispaniola

Yucatán Peninsula

Jamaica

Caribbean Sea

60°W

Pico de Orizaba 18,855 ft (5,747 m) +

Pacific Ocean

Mosquito Coast

Panama Canal

0°

Central America

SOUTH AMERICA

N
W   E
S

EQUATOR

0   800 Miles
0   800 Kilometers

Azimuthal Equidistant Projection

120°W   100°W   80°W

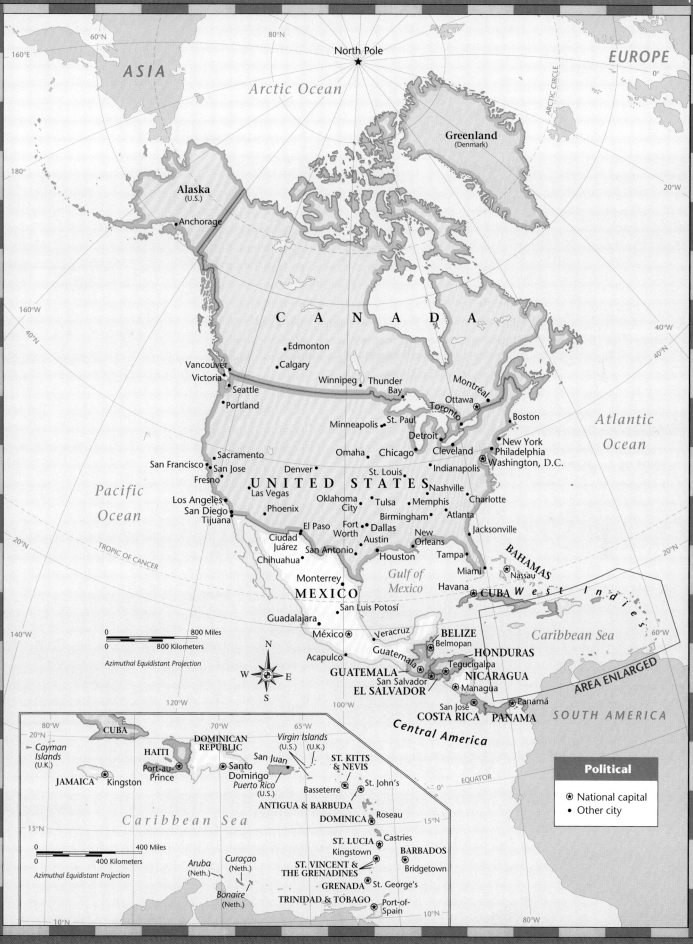

ASIA

EUROPE

60°N   80°N

North Pole

Arctic Ocean

160°E

180°

Greenland
(Denmark)

ARCTIC CIRCLE

20°W

Alaska
(U.S.)

• Anchorage

160°W

C A N A D A

40°N

40°W

40°N

• Edmonton

Vancouver   • Calgary
Victoria   Winnipeg • Thunder   Montréal
• Seattle   Bay
• Portland   St. Paul   Ottawa ⊛   Boston
                        Minneapolis •   Toronto
Pacific   Sacramento •   Omaha   Chicago   Detroit   New York
                San Francisco •   Cleveland   Philadelphia
Ocean   • San Jose   Denver   St. Louis   Indianapolis   Washington, D.C. ⊛
                Fresno •   *Atlantic*
        U N I T E D   S T A T E S   Nashville   *Ocean*
                Los Angeles •   Las Vegas   Oklahoma • Tulsa Memphis •   Charlotte
                San Diego •   Phoenix •   City   Birmingham •   Atlanta
                Tijuana   El Paso   Fort • Dallas   Jacksonville
                Ciudad •   Worth Austin   New
                Juárez   San Antonio •   Orleans   BAHAMAS
                Chihuahua •   Houston   Tampa •
20°N   TROPIC OF CANCER   Miami •   Nassau ⊛   20°N
                          Monterrey •   *Gulf of*   Havana
                M E X I C O   *Mexico*   ⊛ CUBA   *W e s t   I n d i e s*
                         • San Luis Potosí
                Guadalajara •   *Caribbean Sea*   60°W
140°W   0   800 Miles   México ⊛   • Veracruz   BELIZE
           0   800 Kilometers   Guatemala ⊛ Belmopan   AREA ENLARGED
                                      Acapulco •   Tegucigalpa HONDURAS
        Azimuthal Equidistant Projection   ⊛ • Managua NICARAGUA
                          N   GUATEMALA ⊛ San Salvador   *SOUTH AMERICA*
                     W ⊕ E   EL SALVADOR San José ⊛ Panamá ⊛
                          S   COSTA RICA PANAMA
                                          Central America
        120°W   100°W

                                          EQUATOR   0°

        80°W
20°N   CUBA   DOMINICAN   Virgin Islands   **Political**
         Cayman   REPUBLIC   (U.S.) (U.K.)
         Islands   HAITI   San Juan •   ST. KITTS   ⊛ National capital
         (U.K.)   Port-au- ⊛ Santo   & NEVIS
      JAMAICA Kingston Prince   Domingo   ⊛ St. John's   • Other city
                           Puerto Rico Basseterre
                              (U.S.)
                                          ANTIGUA & BARBUDA
        Caribbean Sea   DOMINICA ⊛ Roseau   15°N
15°N
         0   400 Miles   ST. LUCIA ⊛ Castries
         0   400 Kilometers   Kingstown ⊛   BARBADOS
        Azimuthal Equidistant Projection ST. VINCENT &   ⊛ Bridgetown
         Aruba *Curaçao*   THE GRENADINES
         (Neth.) (Neth.)   GRENADA ⊛ St. George's
                Bonaire   TRINIDAD & TOBAGO
                (Neth.)   Port-of-
10°N   Spain   10°N
                           70°W   65°W   80°W

Population Map

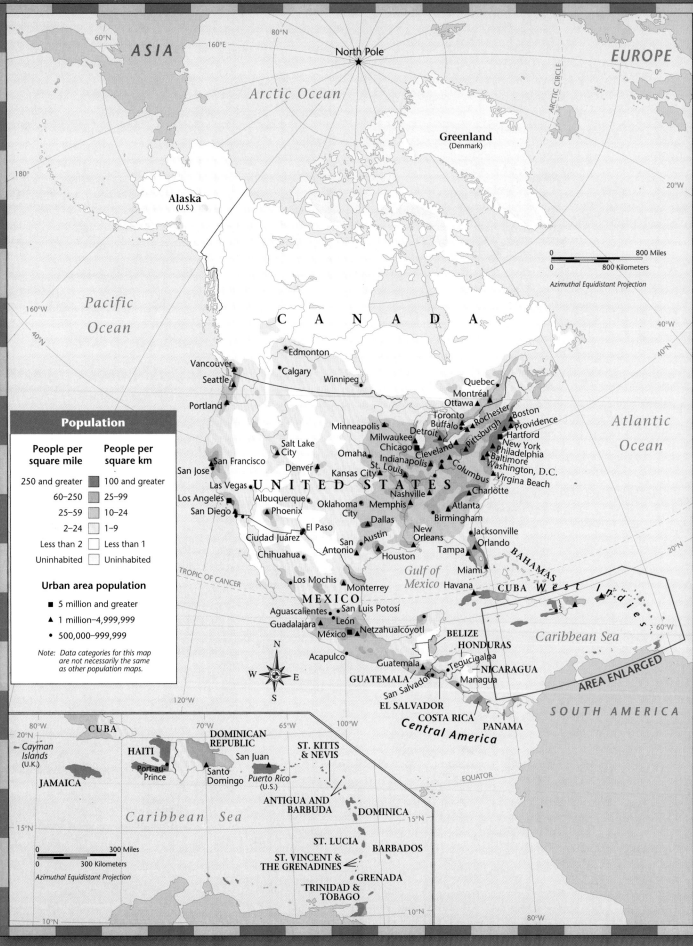

ASIA

North Pole

Arctic Ocean

EUROPE

Greenland
(Denmark)

Alaska
(U.S.)

Pacific
Ocean

CANADA

0   800 Miles
0   800 Kilometers

Azimuthal Equidistant Projection

Edmonton

Vancouver
Seattle
Portland
Calgary
Winnipeg

Quebec
Montréal
Ottawa
Toronto
Buffalo   Rochester Boston
Minneapolis   Pittsburgh Providence
Milwaukee Detroit   New York
Chicago Cleveland Philadelphia
Omaha Indianapolis Baltimore
San Francisco   Columbus Washington, D.C.
St. Louis   Virgina Beach
San Jose   Denver   Kansas City
Las Vegas   UNITED STATES   Charlotte
Los Angeles Albuquerque Nashville Atlanta
San Diego   Phoenix Oklahoma Memphis Birmingham
El Paso   City   Dallas
Ciudad Juárez   New   Jacksonville
Chihuahua   San   Orleans   Orlando
            Antonio Austin   Tampa
Los Mochis Monterrey Houston Miami BAHAMAS
MEXICO   Gulf of   Havana
Aguascalientes San Luis Potosí Mexico CUBA West Indies
Guadalajara León
México   Netzahualcóyotl
Acapulco Guatemala BELIZE
GUATEMALA San Salvador HONDURAS
EL SALVADOR Tegucigalpa NICARAGUA
COSTA RICA Managua
Central America PANAMA

Atlantic
Ocean

Caribbean Sea

AREA ENLARGED

SOUTH AMERICA

TROPIC OF CANCER

Population

People per square mile	People per square km
250 and greater	100 and greater
60–250	25–99
25–59	10–24
2–24	1–9
Less than 2	Less than 1
Uninhabited	Uninhabited

Urban area population

■ 5 million and greater

▲ 1 million–4,999,999

• 500,000–999,999

Note: Data categories for this map are not necessarily the same as other population maps.

N
W   E
S

CUBA
Cayman
Islands
(U.K.)
HAITI
Port-au-
Prince
JAMAICA

DOMINICAN
REPUBLIC
San Juan
Santo
Domingo
Puerto Rico
(U.S.)

ST. KITTS
& NEVIS

ANTIGUA AND
BARBUDA
DOMINICA

Caribbean Sea

ST. LUCIA
ST. VINCENT &
THE GRENADINES

BARBADOS

GRENADA

TRINIDAD &
TOBAGO

EQUATOR

0   300 Miles
0   300 Kilometers

Azimuthal Equidistant Projection

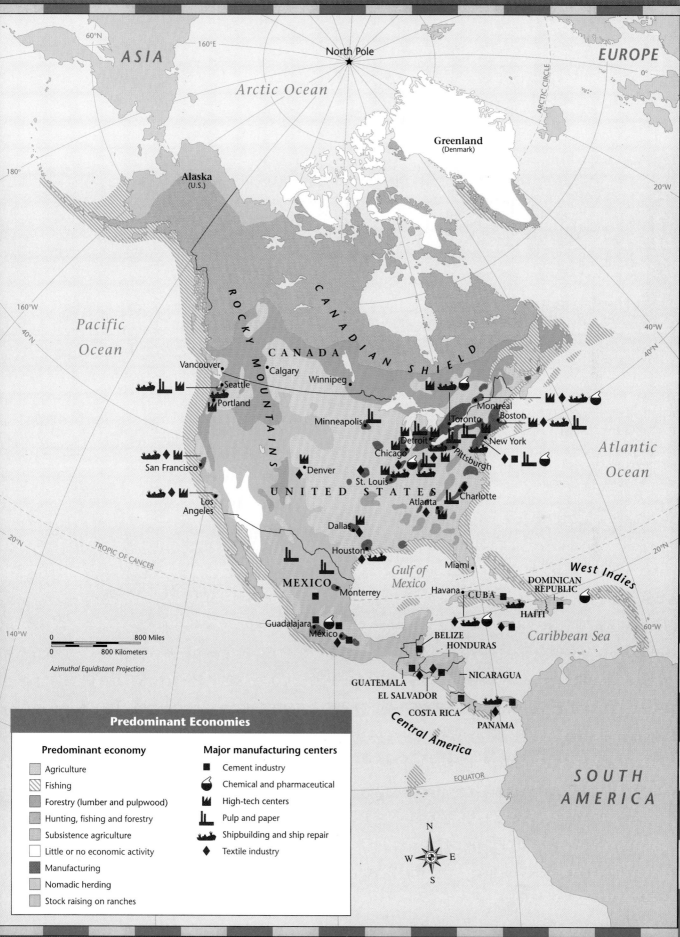

Predominant Economies

Predominant economy

- Agriculture
- Fishing
- Forestry (lumber and pulpwood)
- Hunting, fishing and forestry
- Subsistence agriculture
- Little or no economic activity
- Manufacturing
- Nomadic herding
- Stock raising on ranches

Major manufacturing centers

- ■ Cement industry
- Chemical and pharmaceutical
- High-tech centers
- Pulp and paper
- Shipbuilding and ship repair
- ◆ Textile industry

Azimuthal Equidistant Projection

800 Miles

800 Kilometers

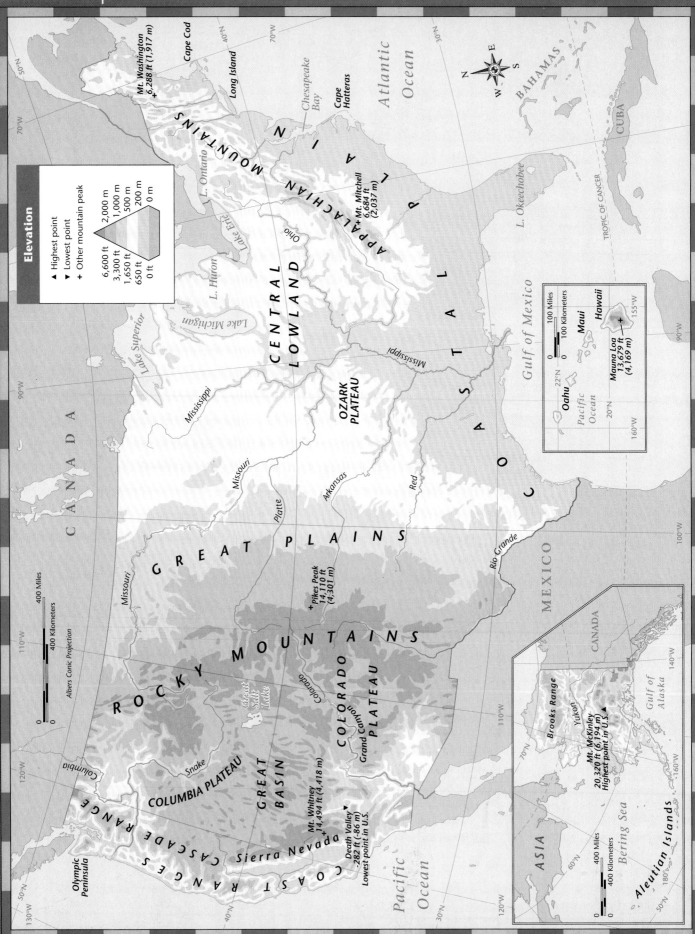

Elevation

▲ Highest point
▼ Lowest point
+ Other mountain peak

6,600 ft	2,000 m
3,300 ft	1,000 m
1,650 ft	500 m
650 ft	200 m
0 ft	0 m

CANADA

Olympic Peninsula

COAST RANGES

CASCADE RANGE

COLUMBIA PLATEAU

Columbia

Snake

GREAT BASIN

Sierra Nevada

Mt. Whitney
14,494 ft (4,418 m) +

Death Valley
-282 ft (-86 m)
Lowest point in U.S. ▼

Great Salt Lake

ROCKY MOUNTAINS

COLORADO PLATEAU

Colorado

Grand Canyon

Pikes Peak
14,110 ft
(4,301 m) +

GREAT PLAINS

Missouri

Platte

Arkansas

Red

Rio Grande

MEXICO

Mississippi

Missouri

Mississippi

OZARK PLATEAU

CENTRAL LOWLAND

Lake Superior

Lake Michigan

L. Huron

Lake Erie

L. Ontario

Ohio

APPALACHIAN MOUNTAINS

Mt. Washington
6,288 ft (1,917 m) +

Cape Cod

Long Island

Chesapeake Bay

Cape Hatteras

COASTAL PLAIN

Atlantic Ocean

Mt. Mitchell
6,684 ft
(2,037 m) +

Gulf of Mexico

L. Okeechobee

TROPIC OF CANCER

BAHAMAS

CUBA

N E S
W

Pacific Ocean

400 Miles
400 Kilometers
0
0
Albers Conic Projection

Hawaii inset

Hawaii

Maui

Oahu

Mauna Loa
13,679 ft
(4,169 m) +

Pacific Ocean

100 Miles
100 Kilometers
0
0

Alaska inset

ASIA

Bering Sea

Aleutian Islands

Gulf of Alaska

CANADA

Brooks Range

Yukon

Mt. McKinley
20,320 ft (6,194 m) ▲
Highest point in U.S.

400 Miles
400 Kilometers
0
0

Political

⊛ National capital
◉ State capital
• Other city

CANADA

MAINE
Augusta
NEW HAMPSHIRE
VERMONT
Montpelier
Concord
MASSACHUSETTS
Boston
Providence
RHODE ISLAND
CONNECTICUT
NEW JERSEY
Hartford
Albany
NEW YORK
Newark
New York
Trenton
Philadelphia
Dover
DELAWARE
MARYLAND
Washington, D.C.
Annapolis
Baltimore
Virginia Beach
Norfolk

Lake Ontario
Rochester
Buffalo
PENNSYLVANIA
Harrisburg
Pittsburgh
WEST VIRGINIA
Charleston
Richmond
VIRGINIA
Raleigh
NORTH CAROLINA
Greensboro
Charlotte
Columbia
SOUTH CAROLINA
Savannah
Jacksonville
FLORIDA
Orlando
Tampa
St. Petersburg
Miami

Lake Huron
Lansing
MICHIGAN
Lake Michigan
Detroit
Toledo
Cleveland
Columbus
OHIO
Indianapolis
Cincinnati
Louisville
Frankfort
KENTUCKY
Nashville
TENNESSEE
Memphis
Atlanta
GEORGIA
Montgomery
ALABAMA
Birmingham
Tallahassee

Lake Superior
WISCONSIN
Milwaukee
Madison
St. Paul
MINNESOTA
Minneapolis
Chicago
ILLINOIS
INDIANA
Springfield
St. Louis
Jefferson City
MISSOURI
ARKANSAS
Little Rock
LOUISIANA
Jackson
MISSISSIPPI
Baton Rouge
New Orleans

Atlantic Ocean

BAHAMAS
N E W S
TROPIC OF CANCER

Gulf of Mexico

HAWAII
Honolulu
Hilo
Pacific Ocean
22°N
20°N
100 Miles
100 Kilometers

IOWA
Des Moines
NORTH DAKOTA
Bismarck
SOUTH DAKOTA
Pierre
NEBRASKA
Omaha
Lincoln
Topeka
KANSAS
Wichita
Kansas City
Tulsa
Oklahoma City
OKLAHOMA
Fort Worth
Dallas
TEXAS
Austin
San Antonio
Houston
El Paso

MEXICO

MONTANA
Helena
WYOMING
Cheyenne
COLORADO
Denver
Santa Fe
Albuquerque
NEW MEXICO

400 Miles
400 Kilometers
Albers Conic Projection

IDAHO
Boise
UTAH
Salt Lake City
ARIZONA
Phoenix
Tucson

NEVADA
Carson City
Las Vegas
San Bernardino
Los Angeles
Long Beach
San Diego
CALIFORNIA
Bakersfield
Fresno
San Jose
Sacramento
San Francisco

WASHINGTON
Seattle
Olympia
OREGON
Salem
Portland

Pacific Ocean

CANADA
Juneau
ALASKA
Fairbanks
Anchorage
Gulf of Alaska
Barrow
Nome
ASIA
Bering Sea

400 Miles
400 Kilometers

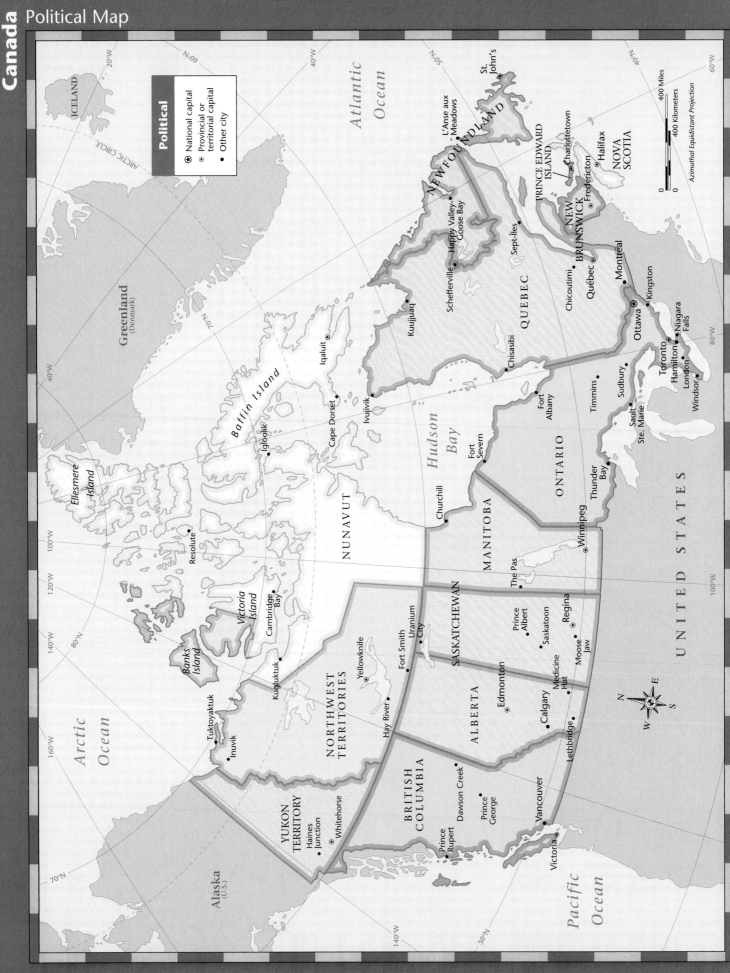

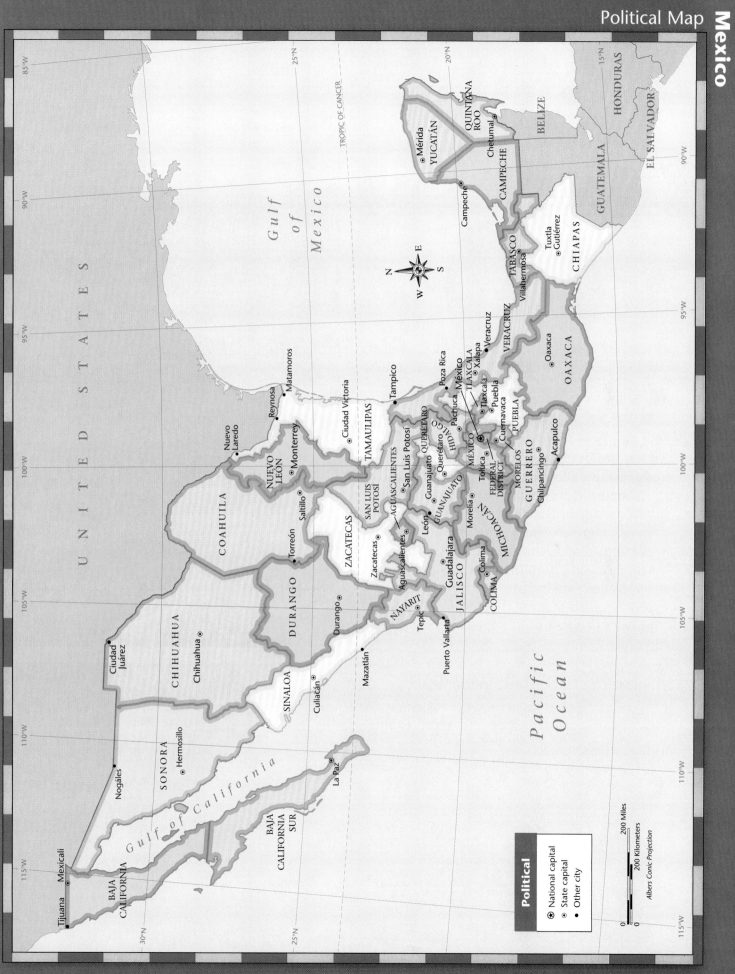

South America

Brazil

Most of South America lies within the tropics, but this does not mean that all places there are the same. The Andes Mountains rise so high that snow and ice cover the mountain peaks, even on the Equator. Hot, steamy rain forests grow on either side of the great Amazon River.

Most people in South America speak Spanish. In Brazil, however, people speak Portuguese, and high in the Andes descendents of the Inca Indians of Peru still speak native languages. More than half of South America's people live in large cities such as Rio de Janeiro.

Tropical Rain Forests Around the World

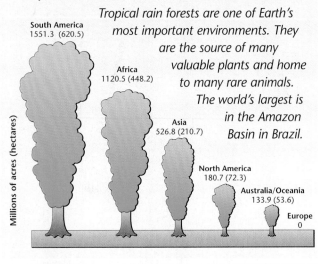

Tropical rain forests are one of Earth's most important environments. They are the source of many valuable plants and home to many rare animals. The world's largest is in the Amazon Basin in Brazil.

Millions of acres (hectares)

South America
1551.3 (620.5)

Africa
1120.5 (448.2)

Asia
526.8 (210.7)

North America
180.7 (72.3)

Australia/Oceania
133.9 (53.6)

Europe
0

Chile

▼ South America's tropical forests are home to many rare animals, such as this gold lion tamarin, which is native to the Amazon Basin.

Brazil

▲Sugar Loaf Mountain towers above the harbor of Rio de Janeiro. This city is famous for its colorful Carnival celebrations.

▶ This girl's bright shawl and felt hat reflect the lasting influence of Peru's cultures.

◀ The Andes Mountains form a rocky spine along the western length of South America. Snow and ice cover many of the peaks.

Peru

Caribbean Sea

Central America

Malpelo I.

Lake Maracaibo

Orinoco

Llanos

GUIANA HIGHLANDS

Angel Falls

AMAZON

Negro

Amazon

Amazon

Marajó I.

EQUATOR

N
W E
S

0°

0°

BASIN

Purus

Madeira

Tapajós

Xingu

Tocantins

São Francisco

Ucayali

10°S

10°S

Lake Titicaca

Mato Grosso Plateau

BRAZILIAN

HIGHLANDS

San Félix I.   San Ambrosio I.

Atacama Desert

Gran Chaco

Paraguay

Iguazú Falls

TROPIC OF CAPRICORN

20°S

20°S

Ojos del Salado
22,572 ft
(6,880 m)

ANDES

PAMPAS

Paraná

Uruguay

Atlantic Ocean

Cerro Aconcagua
22,834 ft (6,960 m)
Highest point in South America

30°S

30°S

Juan Fernández Is.

Río de la Plata

Pacific Ocean

Colorado

Physical

▲ Highest point
▼ Lowest point
+ Other mountain peak

Isla Grande de Chiloé

Valdés Peninsula
-131 ft (-40 m)
Lowest point in South America

0   600 Miles
0   600 Kilometers

40°S

40°S

PATAGONIA

Gulf of San Jorge

Azimuthal Equidistant Projection

Falkland Islands

Strait of Magellan

Tierra del Fuego

South Georgia

50°S

50°S

Cape Horn

80°W   70°W   60°W   50°W

100°W   90°W   80°W   70°W   60°W   50°W   40°W   30°W   20°W

Central America

Caribbean Sea

80°W 70°W 60°W 50°W

Barranquilla
Maracaibo
Caracas
Barquisimeto
Valencia
VENEZUELA
Georgetown
Paramaribo
GUYANA
SURINAME
Cayenne
French Guiana
(France)
Medellín
Bogotá
Cali
COLOMBIA

EQUATOR 0°
Quito
ECUADOR
Guayaquil
Manaus
Belém
EQUATOR 0°
Fortaleza
Natal
Recife
PERU
10°S
Callao
Lima
BOLIVIA
BRAZIL
Salvador
(Bahia)
La Paz
Santa Cruz
Sucre
Goiânia
Brasília
Belo
Horizonte
10°S

PARAGUAY
20°S
Nova Iguaçu
São Paulo
Rio de Janeiro
Santos
Asunción
Curitiba
TROPIC OF CAPRICORN
20°S

CHILE
San Miguel
de Tucumán
Atlantic
Ocean
Pôrto Alegre
Córdoba
Santa
Fe
Rosario
URUGUAY
30°S
Valparaíso Santiago
Buenos Aires
La Plata
Montevideo
30°S

Pacific
Ocean
ARGENTINA
Mar del Plata

N
W   E
S

Political
⊛ National capital
⊙ State capital
• Other city

0   600 Miles
0   600 Kilometers
Azimuthal Equidistant Projection

40°S
40°S

Stanley
Falkland Islands
(U.K.)
South
Georgia
(U.K.)

50°S
50°S

100°W 90°W 80°W 70°W 60°W 50°W 40°W 30°W 20°W

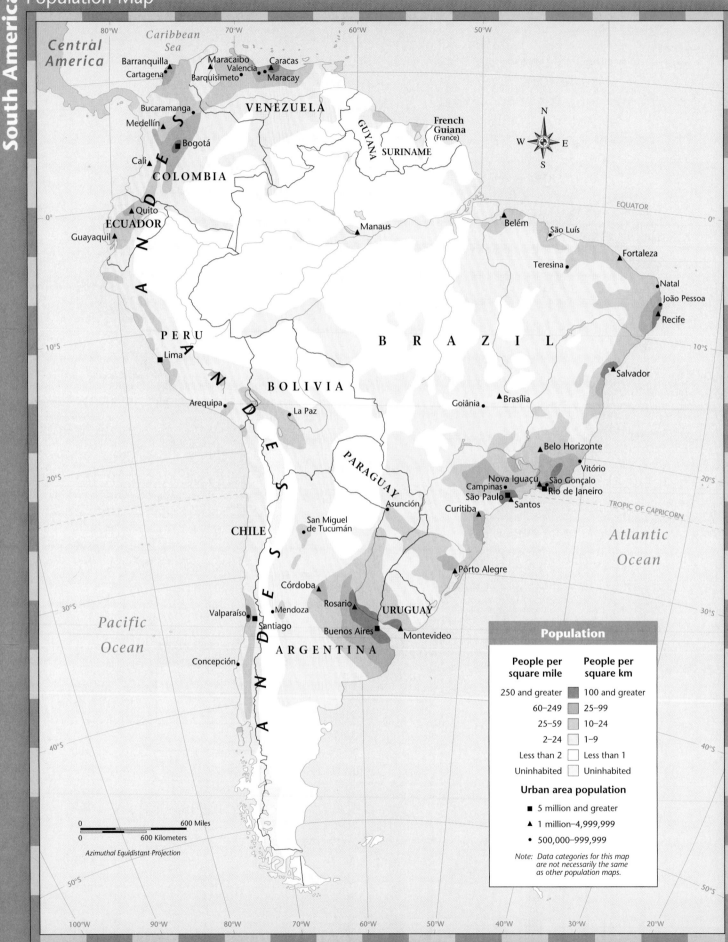

Population Map

Population

People per square mile	People per square km
250 and greater	100 and greater
60–249	25–99
25–59	10–24
2–24	1–9
Less than 2	Less than 1
Uninhabited	Uninhabited

Urban area population

■ 5 million and greater

▲ 1 million–4,999,999

• 500,000–999,999

Note: Data categories for this map are not necessarily the same as other population maps.

600 Miles

600 Kilometers

Azimuthal Equidistant Projection

Central America

Caribbean Sea

Cartagena
Maracaibo
Caracas
VENEZUELA
GUYANA
SURINAME
French Guiana (France)
Bogotá
Cali
COLOMBIA
Quito
ECUADOR
Guayaquil
PERU
AMAZON BASIN
Belém
EQUATOR

N
W E
S

BRAZIL

Lima
BOLIVIA
La Paz

PARAGUAY

Rio de Janeiro
São Paulo
TROPIC OF CAPRICORN

Atlantic Ocean

CHILE

Rosario
URUGUAY
Buenos Aires
Montevideo

Pacific Ocean

Santiago
ARGENTINA

Concepción

ANDES

PATAGONIA

0   600 Miles
0   600 Kilometers
Azimuthal Equidistant Projection

Predominant Economies

Predominant economy

- Agriculture
- Fishing
- Forestry (lumber and pulpwood)
- Subsistence agriculture
- Little or no economic activity
- Manufacturing
- Stock raising on ranges

Major manufacturing centers

- Cement industry
- Chemical and pharmaceutical
- High-tech centers
- Pulp and paper
- Shipbuilding and ship repair
- Textile industry

Africa

Africa is a continent of diverse environments and people. In the deserts of northern and southern Africa people move from place to place in search of water. Near the equator, in the rain forests of the Congo River Basin, water is abundant. The grasslands of East Africa, called savannas, are home to herds of wild animals, including elephants, lions, zebras, and wildebeests.

Most people in Africa farm lands in the river valleys and along the coastal plains where there is access to markets for trading. Many African cities are growing, as people move from farm areas to find jobs.

Sources of the World's Diamonds

Diamonds are desired because of their beauty and hardness. Half of all diamonds in the world come from Africa, especially central and southern Africa.

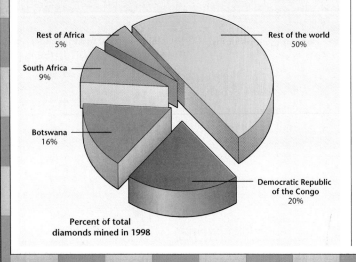

Rest of Africa
5%

South Africa
9%

Botswana
16%

Rest of the world
50%

Democratic Republic
of the Congo
20%

Percent of total
diamonds mined in 1998

▲ An elephant walks through the dry lands of southern Kenya. In the distance is the snow-covered summit of Africa's highest peak, Mount Kilimanjaro, in Tanzania.

▶ In this busy market in North Africa, people dressed in turbans and long robes show the influence of Arab culture.

Egypt

▼ *Training to become a diamond expert, a student closely examines uncut, unpolished diamonds from mines in Central African Republic.*

Central African Republic

► *Colorful jewelry adorns these young Masai women. People of East Africa's Masai tribe mainly herd cattle for a living.*

Kenya

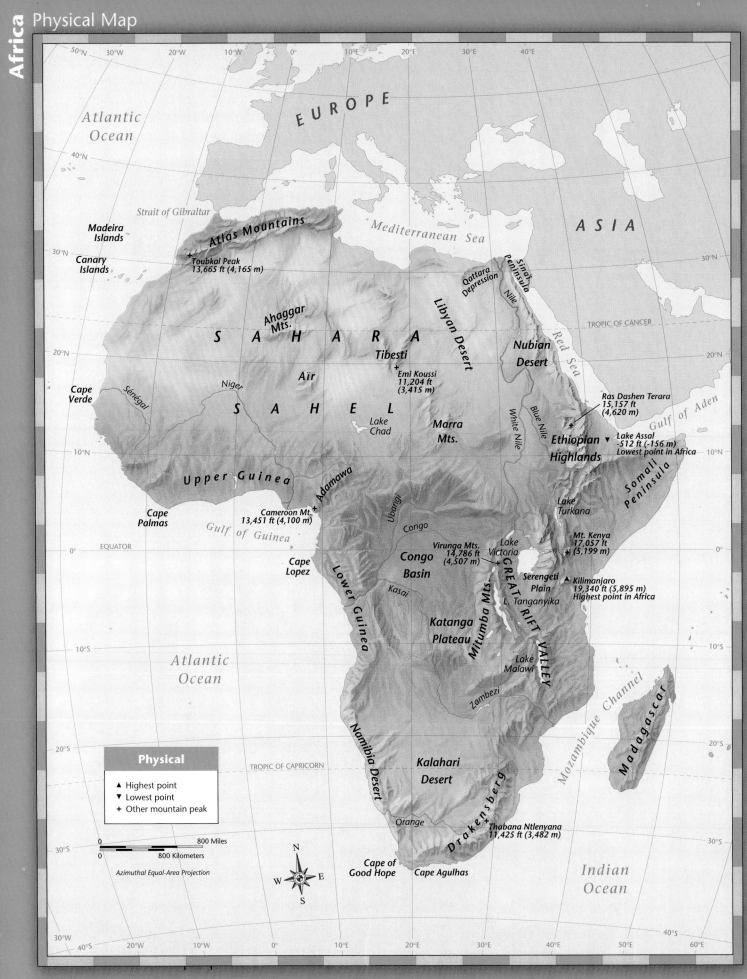

EUROPE

ASIA

Atlantic
Ocean

Mediterranean Sea

Strait of Gibraltar

Madeira
Islands

Canary
Islands

Atlas Mountains
+ Toubkal Peak
13,665 ft (4,165 m)

Qattara
Depression

Sinai
Peninsula

Nile

TROPIC OF CANCER

Ahaggar
Mts.

S A H A R A

Libyan
Desert

Nubian
Desert

Red Sea

Tibesti
+ Emi Koussi
11,204 ft
(3,415 m)

Aïr

Niger

S A H E L

Ras Dashen Terara
15,157 ft
(4,620 m)

Gulf of Aden

Cape
Verde

Sénégal

Lake
Chad

Marra
Mts.

White Nile

Blue Nile

Ethiopian ▼
Highlands

Lake Assal
-512 ft (-156 m)
Lowest point in Africa

Upper Guinea

Somali
Peninsula

+ Adamawa

Cameroon Mt. +
13,451 ft (4,100 m)

Cape
Palmas

Gulf of Guinea

Ubangi

Congo

Lake
Turkana

Mt. Kenya
17,057 ft
+ (5,199 m)

EQUATOR

0°

Cape
Lopez

Virunga Mts.
14,786 ft
(4,507 m)

Congo
Basin

Lake
Victoria

GREAT RIFT VALLEY

Kilimanjaro
▲ 19,340 ft (5,895 m)
Highest point in Africa

Kasai

Mitumba Mts.

Serengeti
Plain

L. Tanganyika

Lower Guinea

Katanga
Plateau

Lake
Malawi

Atlantic
Ocean

Zambezi

Mozambique Channel

Madagascar

Namibia Desert

TROPIC OF CAPRICORN

Kalahari
Desert

Drakensberg

Orange

Thabana Ntlenyana
+ 11,425 ft (3,482 m)

Cape of
Good Hope

Cape Agulhas

Indian
Ocean

N
W   E
S

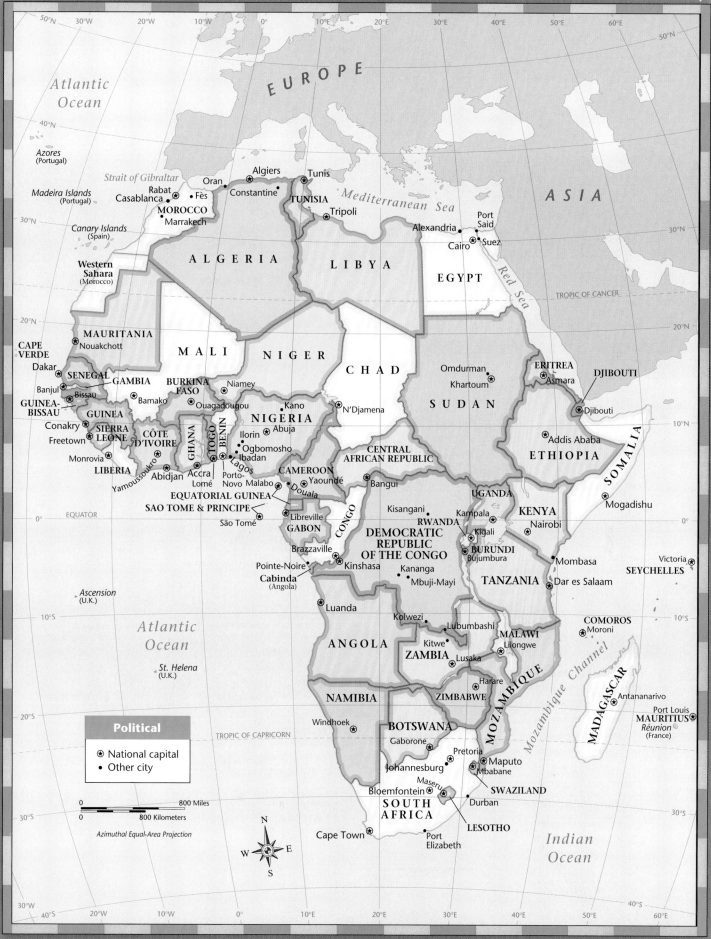

Atlantic
Ocean

EUROPE

ASIA

*Azores
(Portugal)*

Strait of Gibraltar

Oran   Algiers   Tunis
Rabat   Fès   Constantine
Casablanca   TUNISIA
MOROCCO   Tripoli
Marrakech

*Madeira Islands
(Portugal)*

Mediterranean Sea

Port
Said
Alexandria   30°N
Cairo   Suez

*Canary Islands
(Spain)*

ALGERIA   LIBYA   EGYPT

Red Sea

**Western
Sahara**
(Morocco)

TROPIC OF CANCER

20°N   20°N

MAURITANIA

MALI   NIGER   CHAD

Nouakchott

Omdurman   ERITREA   DJIBOUTI
Khartoum   Asmara

**CAPE
VERDE**

Dakar   SUDAN   Djibouti
SENEGAL   GAMBIA   BURKINA
Banjul   Bamako   FASO   Niamey
Bissau   Ouagadougou   Kano
**GUINEA-
BISSAU**   N'Djamena
GUINEA   NIGERIA
Conakry   Abuja   Addis Ababa
SIERRA   Ilorin
Freetown   LEONE   CÔTE   GHANA   Ogbomosho   CENTRAL   ETHIOPIA   SOMALIA
Monrovia   D'IVOIRE   TOGO   Ibadan   AFRICAN REPUBLIC
LIBERIA   BENIN
Yamoussoukro   Accra   Lagos   CAMEROON   Bangui   UGANDA   Mogadishu
Abidjan   Lomé   Porto-   Malabo   Yaoundé   KENYA
Novo   Douala   Kisangani   Kampala
EQUATORIAL GUINEA   Nairobi
SAO TOME & PRINCIPE   CONGO   RWANDA   Kigali
Libreville   DEMOCRATIC   Kigali   BURUNDI
São Tomé   GABON   REPUBLIC   Bujumbura
OF THE CONGO   Mombasa   SEYCHELLES

EQUATOR   0°   0°

Brazzaville   TANZANIA
Pointe-Noire   Kinshasa   Kananga   Dar es Salaam
Cabinda   Mbuji-Mayi
(Angola)

*Ascension
(U.K.)*

Luanda   COMOROS
Kolwezi   Moroni
Atlantic   Lubumbashi
Ocean   ANGOLA   Kitwe   MALAWI
ZAMBIA   Lilongwe
*St. Helena
(U.K.)*   Lusaka   MADAGASCAR

Harare   MOZAMBIQUE   Antananarivo
NAMIBIA   ZIMBABWE   Port Louis
MAURITIUS
*Réunion
(France)*

20°S   Windhoek   TROPIC OF CAPRICORN   BOTSWANA   20°S

Gaborone
Political   Pretoria
Maputo
⊛ National capital   Johannesburg   Mbabane
• Other city   Maseru   SWAZILAND
Bloemfontein   Durban
SOUTH   LESOTHO
AFRICA
0   800 Miles
0   800 Kilometers   Cape Town   Port   Indian
Elizabeth   Ocean

Azimuthal Equal-Area Projection

N
W   E
S

29

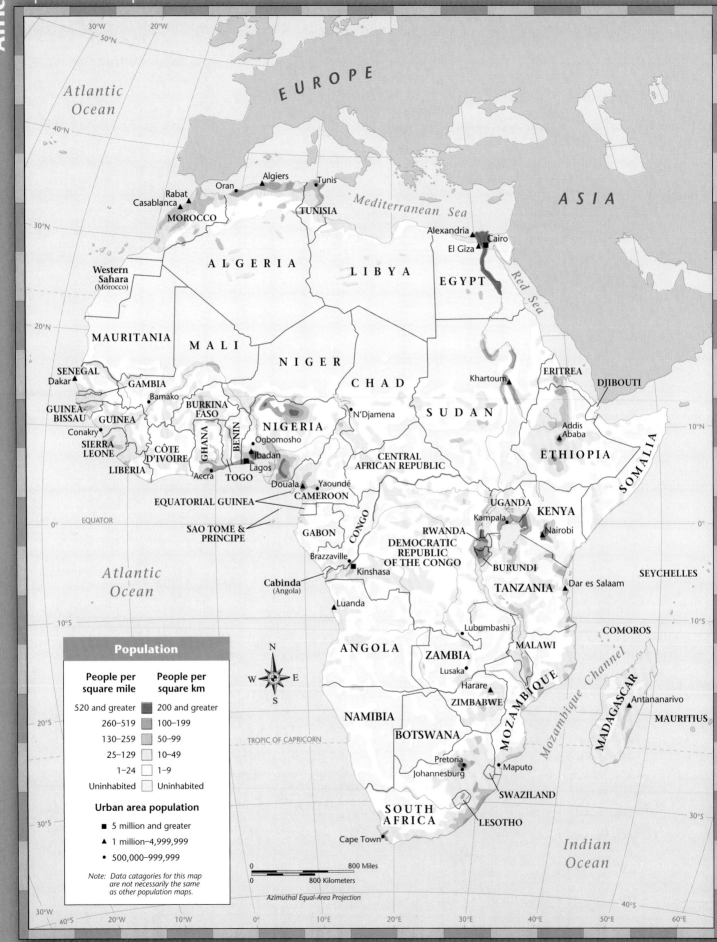

Population

People per square mile | **People per square km**
520 and greater | 200 and greater
260–519 | 100–199
130–259 | 50–99
25–129 | 10–49
1–24 | 1–9
Uninhabited | Uninhabited

Urban area population
■ 5 million and greater
▲ 1 million–4,999,999
• 500,000–999,999

Note: Data catagories for this map are not necessarily the same as other population maps.

0   800 Miles
0   800 Kilometers

Azimuthal Equal-Area Projection

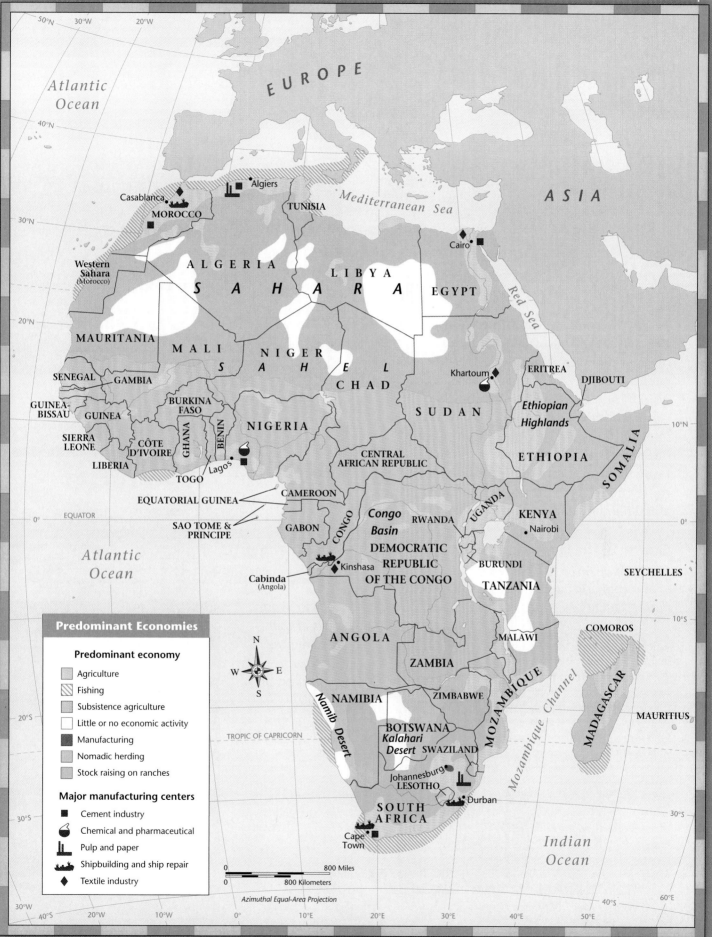

Predominant Economies

Predominant economy

- Agriculture
- Fishing
- Subsistence agriculture
- Little or no economic activity
- Manufacturing
- Nomadic herding
- Stock raising on ranches

Major manufacturing centers

- ■ Cement industry
- ◗ Chemical and pharmaceutical
- ⊥ Pulp and paper
- ⛴ Shipbuilding and ship repair
- ◆ Textile industry

0   800 Miles
0   800 Kilometers

Azimuthal Equal-Area Projection

Europe

From the sunny beaches of the Mediterranean Sea to the icy shores of the Arctic Ocean, Europe is a continent of great diversity. Historically, Europe has been home to great empires such as the Roman and the Greek. Countries like Germany have been divided by wars and reunited in peace. People of Europe speak different languages, celebrate different holidays, enjoy different foods, live in more than 40 countries–all in an area just a little larger than the United States.

Growth of the European Union

The European Union (EU) has united the economies of 15 countries. In the near future 13 more countries are expected to join.

Sweden
Finland
Austria
Portugal
Spain
Greece
United Kingdom
Ireland
Denmark
Netherlands
Luxembourg
Italy
France
Germany
Belgium

1995 (3)
1986 (2)
1981 (1)
1973 (3)
1951 (6)

1950 1960 1970 1980 1990 2000

New members Existing members

Italy

▲*Long, warm days of the Mediterranean summer help sunflowers grow in Italy.*

Croatia

▼ St. Basil's Cathedral is a famous Russian landmark. Located in the city of Moscow, it is a symbol of the Russian Orthodox Church.

Russia

◄ In towns and cities across Europe, people often shop in open markets—like this one in Croatia.

▶ The changing of the guard at London's Buckingham Palace is a popular tourist attraction.

United Kingdom

ASIA

URAL MOUNTAINS

Europe-Asia Boundary

Ural

Pechora

Kama

Kama

Volga

Volga

Don

-92 ft (-28 m) Lowest point in Europe

Elbrus 18,510 ft (5,642 m) Highest point in Europe

Caspian Sea

CAUCASUS MOUNTAINS

Crimea

Don

Sea of Azov

Black Sea

Bosporus

Sea of Marmara

Dardanelles

A commonly accepted division between Asia and Europe—here marked by a maroon, dashed line—is formed by the Ural Mountains, Ural River, Caspian Sea, Caucasus Mountains, and the Black Sea with its outlets, the Bosporus and Dardanelles.

Northern Dvina

Lake Onega

Lake Ladoga

Central Russian Upland

Dnieper

Dniester

Aegean Sea

Crete

Barents Sea

Kola Peninsula

Lake Region

Western Dvina

NORTHERN EUROPEAN PLAIN

Carpathian Mts.

Danube

Balkan

Balkan Mts.

Peloponnesus

Peninsula

White Sea

North Cape

LAPLAND

Gulf of Finland

Vistula

Oder

Ionian Sea

Adriatic Sea

SCANDINAVIAN PENINSULA

Gulf of Bothnia

Baltic Sea

Elbe

Danube

Apennines

+Etna 10,902 ft (3,323 m)

Tyrrhenian Sea

Sicily

Zealand

Jutland Peninsula

Ruhr Valley

Rhine

ALPS

Po

Riviera

Ligurian Sea

Corsica

Sardinia

Mediterranean Sea

AFRICA

Norwegian Sea

ARCTIC CIRCLE

PRIME MERIDIAN

Faroe Islands

Shetland Islands

Orkney Islands

Highlands

Outer Hebrides

Great Britain

North Sea

Seine

Loire

Brittany

Massif Central

+Mt. Blanc 15,771 ft (4,807 m)

Rhône

Pyrenees

Ebro

Balearic Is.

Balearic Sea

Iceland

Ireland

Irish Sea

British Isles

Celtic Sea

English Channel

Bay of Biscay

Cantabrian Mts.

Douro

Iberian Peninsula

Tagus

Baetic Mts.

Strait of Gibraltar

Atlantic Ocean

Physical
▲ Highest point
▼ Lowest point
+ Other mountain peak

600 Miles

600 Kilometers

Azimuthal Equidistant Projection

A commonly accepted division between Asia and Europe—here marked by a maroon, dashed line—is formed by the Ural Mountains, Ural River, Caspian Sea, Caucasus Mountains, and the Black Sea with its outlets, the Bosporus and Dardanelles.

Political

⊛ National capital
• Other city
□ Small country

600 Miles
600 Kilometers
Azimuthal Equidistant Projection

35

Population Map

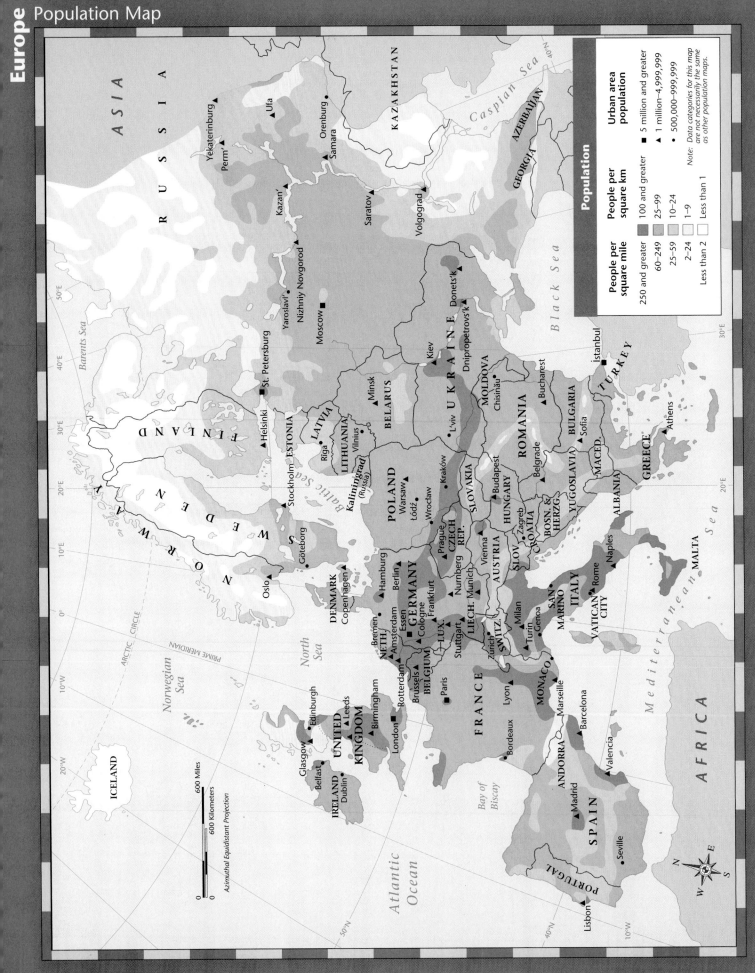

Population

People per square mile	People per square km
250 and greater	100 and greater
60–249	25–99
25–59	10–24
2–24	1–9
Less than 2	Less than 1

Urban area population

■ 5 million and greater
▲ 1 million–4,999,999
● 500,000–999,999

Note: Data categories for this map are not necessarily the same as other population maps.

ASIA

RUSSIA

KAZAKHSTAN

Caspian Sea

Yekaterinburg
Perm'
Ufa
Orenburg
Samara
Kazan'
Saratov
Volgograd

AZERBAIJAN
GEORGIA

Yaroslavl'
Nizhniy Novgorod
Moscow

St. Petersburg

FINLAND

Helsinki

ESTONIA
LATVIA
Riga
LITHUANIA
Vilnius
Kaliningrad (Russia)

BELARUS
Minsk

Kiev
L'viv UKRAINE
Dnipropetrovs'k
Donets'k

MOLDOVA
Chisinău

Black Sea

Istanbul
TURKEY

Barents Sea

NORWAY

SWEDEN

Stockholm

Göteborg

Oslo

Baltic Sea

POLAND
Warsaw
Łódź
Wrocław
Kraków

Prague
CZECH REP.
SLOVAKIA
Budapest
HUNGARY

Zagreb
CROATIA
SLOV.
BOSN. & HERZ.
YUGOSLAVIA
Belgrade
ROMANIA
Bucharest
BULGARIA
Sofia
MACED.
ALBANIA

GREECE
Athens

Mediterranean Sea

ICELAND

Norwegian Sea

ARCTIC CIRCLE

PRIME MERIDIAN

North Sea

DENMARK
Copenhagen

Bremen
Hamburg
Berlin
Essen
Amsterdam
NETH.
Cologne
GERMANY
Frankfurt
Nürnberg
LIECH. Munich
Stuttgart
LUX.
BELGIUM
Brussels
Rotterdam

Zurich
SWITZ.
AUSTRIA
Vienna
SLOV.

Milan
Turin
Genoa
SAN MARINO
ITALY
Rome
VATICAN CITY
Naples

MONACO
Lyon
Marseille

FRANCE

Paris

Bay of Biscay

Bordeaux

ANDORRA
SPAIN
Madrid
Barcelona
Valencia
Seville

PORTUGAL
Lisbon

MALTA

AFRICA

UNITED KINGDOM
Glasgow
Edinburgh
Leeds
Birmingham
London

IRELAND
Belfast
Dublin

Atlantic Ocean

600 Miles
600 Kilometers
Azimuthal Equidistant Projection

N
W E
S

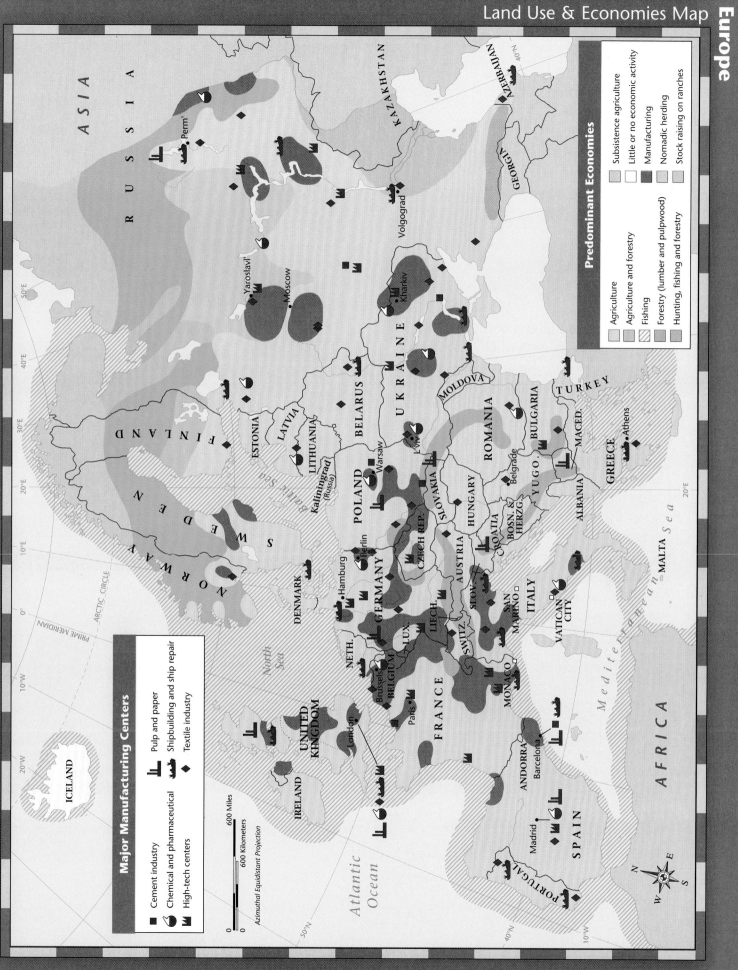

Major Manufacturing Centers

- Cement industry
- Chemical and pharmaceutical
- High-tech centers
- Pulp and paper
- Shipbuilding and ship repair
- Textile industry

600 Miles

600 Kilometers

Azimuthal Equidistant Projection

Predominant Economies

- Agriculture
- Agriculture and forestry
- Fishing
- Forestry (lumber and pulpwood)
- Hunting, fishing and forestry
- Subsistence agriculture
- Little or no economic activity
- Manufacturing
- Nomadic herding
- Stock raising on ranches

ICELAND

A S I A

R U S S I A

Perm'

Yaroslavl'

Moscow

Volgograd

Kharkiv

KAZAKHSTAN

AZERBAIJAN

GEORGIA

TURKEY

ASIA

N O R W A Y

S W E D E N

F I N L A N D

ESTONIA

LATVIA

LITHUANIA

Baltic Sea

Kaliningrad
(Russia)

BELARUS

U K R A I N E

MOLDOVA

ROMANIA

BULGARIA

YUGO.

MACED.

ALBANIA

GREECE

Athens

POLAND

Warsaw

Berlin

Hamburg

DENMARK

North
Sea

NETH.

GERMANY

CZECH REP.

SLOVAKIA

AUSTRIA

HUNGARY

CROATIA

BOSN. &
HERZ.

SLOV.

LIECH.

SWITZ.

ITALY

SAN
MARINO

VATICAN
CITY

Belgrade

Lviv

UNITED
KINGDOM

London

IRELAND

Atlantic
Ocean

Brussels

BELGIUM

LUX.

Paris

F R A N C E

MONACO

ANDORRA

Barcelona

Madrid

S P A I N

PORTUGAL

AFRICA

Mediterranean Sea

MALTA

ARCTIC CIRCLE

PRIME MERIDIAN

N
E
S
W

Asia

Asia is Earth's largest continent and home to more than 60 percent of the world's people. It is a continent of extremes. Mount Everest, in Nepal, is the highest mountain on Earth. The shore of the Dead Sea, in Israel, is the lowest place on land. The Arabian Peninsula is a vast, dry desert, but Indonesia has steamy rainforests. With over one billion people, China has the world's largest population.

Religions of the World

Many of the world's major religions began in Asia. From there, they spread across the world. This graph shows the percent of the world's population that identifies with each of these major religions.

Belief not originating in Asia
19%

Other*
1%

Islam
20%

Hinduism
14%

Buddhism
6%

Christianity
33%

Confucianism/ Chinese traditional religions
7%

* includes Judaism, Sikhism, Bahai, and religions less than 0.1%

Laos

▲ *A river becomes a highway for this floating market. People move about to trade and sell their goods.*

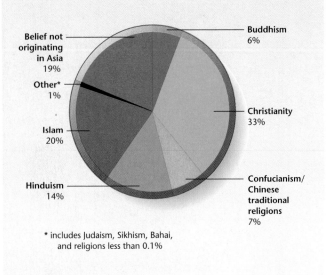

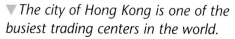

▼ The city of Hong Kong is one of the busiest trading centers in the world.

China

Pakistan

◀ Climbers seem tiny below towering peaks and jagged glaciers of the Karakoram Mountains.

▶ This elephant in northwest India is draped in colorful blankets. Indian elephants can be trained to work and carry heavy loads.

India

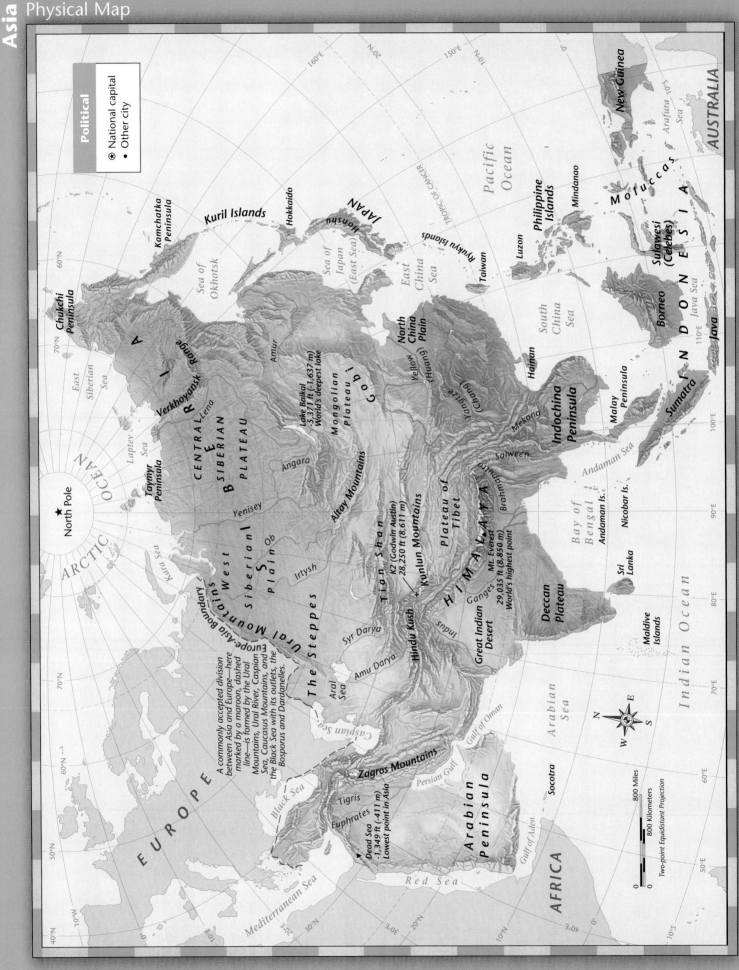

Political
⊛ National capital
• Other city

New Guinea

AUSTRALIA

Arafura 10°S
Sea

Moluccas

Philippine
Islands

Mindanao

INDONESIA

Sulawesi
(Celebes)

Kamchatka
Peninsula

Kuril Islands

Hokkaido

JAPAN
Honshu

Luzon

Taiwan

Ryukyu Islands

Borneo

Java Sea

Chukchi
Peninsula

Sea of
Okhotsk

Sea of
Japan
(East Sea)

East
China
Sea

North
China
Plain

Hainan

Malay
Peninsula

Indochina
Peninsula

Sumatra

Java

East
Siberian
Sea

Verkhoyansk Range

Amur

Yellow
(Huang)

Yangtze
(Chang)

South
China
Sea

CENTRAL
SIBERIAN
PLATEAU

Lake Baikal
-5,371 ft (-1,637 m)
World's deepest lake

Mongolian
Plateau

Gobi

Mekong

Andaman Sea

Laptev
Sea

Lena

Taymyr
Peninsula

Angara

Altay Mountains

Salween

Brahmaputra

Bay of
Bengal

Andaman Is.

Nicobar Is.

ARCTIC OCEAN

North Pole

Kara Sea

Yenisey

Ob

West
Siberian
Plain

Irtysh

Tian Shan

K2 (Godwin Austin)
28,250 ft (8,611 m)

Kunlun Mountains

Plateau of
Tibet

HIMALAYA

Mt. Everest
29,035 ft (8,850 m)
World's highest point

Indus

Ganges

Deccan
Plateau

Sri
Lanka

Maldive
Islands

Indian Ocean

Ural Mountains

The Steppes

Syr Darya

Amu Darya

Aral
Sea

Hindu Kush

Great Indian
Desert

A commonly accepted division
between Asia and Europe—here
marked by a maroon, dashed
line—is formed by the Ural
Mountains, Ural River, Caspian
Sea, Caucasus Mountains, and
the Black Sea with its outlets, the
Bosporus and Dardanelles.

Europe-Asia Boundary

EUROPE

Black Sea

Caspian Sea

Zagros Mountains

Tigris

Euphrates

Dead Sea
-1,349 ft (-411 m)
Lowest point in Asia

Persian Gulf

Gulf of Oman

Arabian
Sea

Arabian
Peninsula

Socotra

Gulf of Aden

Red Sea

Mediterranean Sea

AFRICA

N
W · E
S

800 Miles

800 Kilometers

Two-point Equidistant Projection

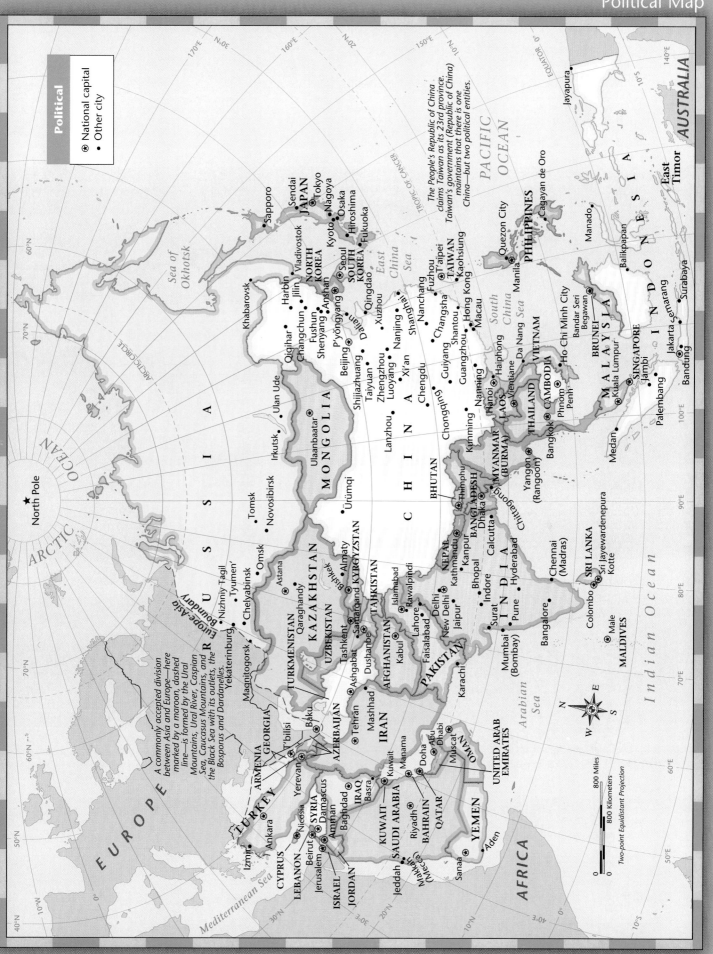

Political
- ⊛ National capital
- • Other city

ARCTIC OCEAN

North Pole

Sea of Okhotsk

Europe-Asia Boundary

A commonly accepted division between Asia and Europe—here marked by a maroon, dashed line—is formed by the Ural Mountains, Ural River, Caspian Sea, Caucasus Mountains, and the Black Sea with its outlets, the Bosporus and Dardanelles.

The People's Republic of China claims Taiwan as its 23rd province. Taiwan's government (Republic of China) maintains that there is one China—but two political entities.

PACIFIC OCEAN

TROPIC OF CANCER

EQUATOR 0°

R U S S I A

EUROPE

Khabarovsk

Sapporo
Sendai
JAPAN
Tokyo
Nagoya
Osaka
Kyoto
Hiroshima
Fukuoka

Vladivostok
NORTH KOREA
P'yŏngyang
Seoul
SOUTH KOREA
Jilin
Harbin
Changchun
Fushun
Shenyang Anshan
Qiqihar
Beijing
Dalian
Qingdao
East China Sea

Ulan Ude
Irkutsk
Tomsk
Novosibirsk
Omsk
Astana
Chelyabinsk
Tyumen'
Yekaterinburg
Nizhniy Tagil
Magnitogorsk

MONGOLIA
Ulaanbaatar ⊛

Ürümqi

C H I N A
Lanzhou
Xi'an
Chengdu
Chongqing
Guiyang
Kunming
Nanning
Guangzhou
Hong Kong
Macau
Shantou
Changsha
Nanchang
Fuzhou
T'aipei ⊛
TAIWAN
Kaohsiung
Shanghai
Nanjing
Luoyang
Zhengzhou
Xuzhou
Shijiazhuang
Taiyuan

Quezon City
PHILIPPINES
Manila ⊛
Cagayan de Oro

Jayapura

AUSTRALIA
East Timor

I N D O N E S I A
Manado
Balikpapan
Surabaya
Semarang
Bandung
Jakarta ⊛
Palembang
Jambi
Medan

SINGAPORE ⊛
MALAYSIA
Kuala Lumpur ⊛
BRUNEI
Bandar Seri Begawan ⊛

VIETNAM
Ho Chi Minh City
Da Nang
Haiphong
Hanoi ⊛
Vientiane ⊛
LAOS
CAMBODIA
Phnom Penh ⊛
THAILAND
Bangkok ⊛
MYANMAR (BURMA)
Yangon (Rangoon)

Chittagong
BANGLADESH
Dhaka ⊛
BHUTAN
Thimphu ⊛
NEPAL
Kathmandu ⊛
Calcutta

KAZAKHSTAN
Qaraghandy
Bishkek ⊛
KYRGYZSTAN
Almaty
Tashkent ⊛
UZBEKISTAN
Samarqand
TAJIKISTAN
Dushanbe ⊛
TURKMENISTAN
Ashgabat ⊛
AFGHANISTAN
Kabul ⊛

PAKISTAN
Islamabad ⊛
Rawalpindi
Lahore
Faisalabad
Karachi

I N D I A
New Delhi ⊛
Delhi
Jaipur
Kanpur
Bhopal
Indore
Surat
Mumbai (Bombay)
Pune
Hyderabad
Bangalore
Chennai (Madras)

SRI LANKA
Sri Jayewardenepura Kotte ⊛
Colombo
Male ⊛
MALDIVES

Indian Ocean

IRAN
Tehrān ⊛
Mashhad

Baku ⊛
AZERBAIJAN
ARMENIA
Yerevan ⊛
GEORGIA
T'bilisi ⊛

TURKEY
Ankara ⊛
Izmir
CYPRUS
Nicosia ⊛
LEBANON
Beirut ⊛
Damascus ⊛
SYRIA
ISRAEL
Jerusalem ⊛
Amman ⊛
JORDAN

Baghdad ⊛
IRAQ
Basra
KUWAIT
Kuwait ⊛
SAUDI ARABIA
Riyadh ⊛
Jeddah
Makkah (Mecca) ⊛

BAHRAIN
Manama ⊛
QATAR
Doha ⊛
Abu Dhabi ⊛
UNITED ARAB EMIRATES
OMAN
Muscat ⊛
YEMEN
Sanaa ⊛
Aden

Arabian Sea

Mediterranean Sea

AFRICA

Black Sea

800 Miles
800 Kilometers
0
0
Two-point Equidistant Projection

N
W — E
S

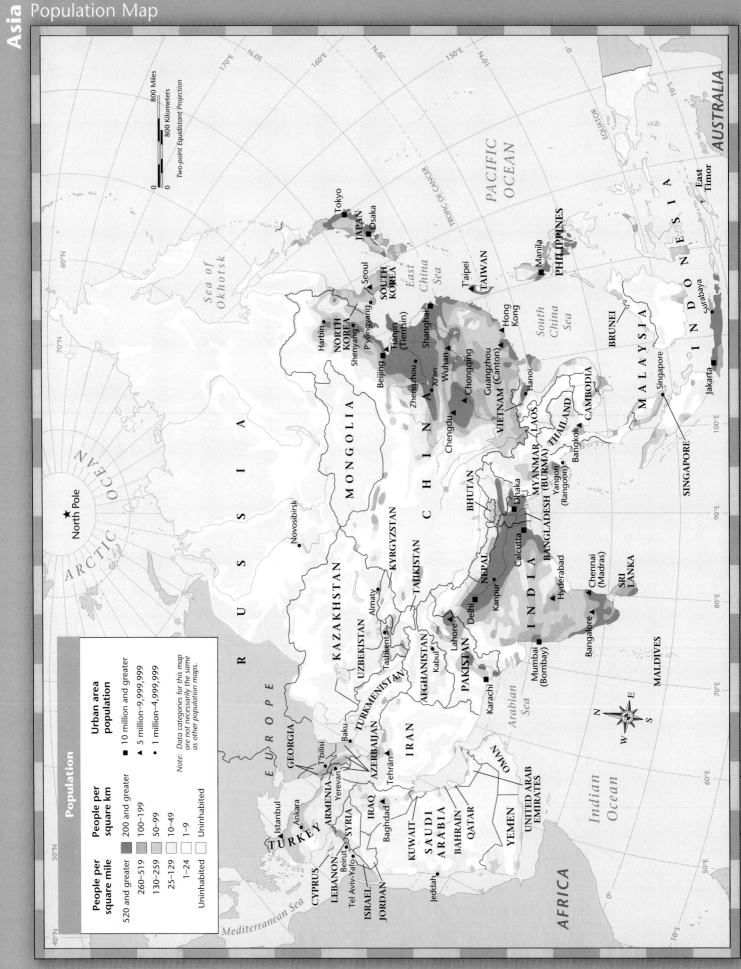

Population

People per square mile	People per square km
520 and greater	200 and greater
260–519	100–199
130–259	50–99
25–129	10–49
1–24	1–9
Uninhabited	Uninhabited

Urban area population
- ■ 10 million and greater
- ▲ 5 million–9,999,999
- • 1 million–4,999,999

Note: Data categories for this map are not necessarily the same as other population maps.

800 Miles
800 Kilometers
Two-point Equidistant Projection

ARCTIC OCEAN
North Pole

RUSSIA
EUROPE
AFRICA

Sea of Okhotsk
PACIFIC OCEAN
East China Sea
South China Sea
Arabian Sea
Indian Ocean
Mediterranean Sea

TROPIC OF CANCER
EQUATOR

Tokyo
Osaka
JAPAN
Seoul
SOUTH KOREA
P'yongyang
NORTH KOREA
Harbin
Shenyang
Beijing
Tianjin (Tientsin)
Zhengzhou
Xi'an
Wuhan
Chengdu
Chongqing
Shanghai
Guangzhou (Canton)
Hong Kong
Hanoi
Taipei
TAIWAN
Manila
PHILIPPINES
BRUNEI
MALAYSIA
Singapore
SINGAPORE
INDONESIA
Jakarta
Surabaya
East Timor
AUSTRALIA

CHINA
MONGOLIA
Novosibirsk
KAZAKHSTAN
KYRGYZSTAN
TAJIKISTAN
UZBEKISTAN
Tashkent
Almaty
TURKMENISTAN
AFGHANISTAN
Kabul
PAKISTAN
Lahore
Karachi
Delhi
Kanpur
INDIA
Mumbai (Bombay)
Hyderabad
Bangalore
Chennai (Madras)
SRI LANKA
MALDIVES
NEPAL
BHUTAN
BANGLADESH
Dhaka
Calcutta
MYANMAR (BURMA)
Yangon (Rangoon)
LAOS
THAILAND
Bangkok
CAMBODIA
VIETNAM

Baku
AZERBAIJAN
ARMENIA
Yerevan
GEORGIA
T'bilisi
IRAN
Tehrân
IRAQ
Baghdad
SYRIA
Beirut
LEBANON
Istanbul
Ankara
TURKEY
CYPRUS
ISRAEL
Tel Aviv-Yafo
JORDAN
KUWAIT
SAUDI ARABIA
BAHRAIN
QATAR
UNITED ARAB EMIRATES
OMAN
YEMEN
Jeddah

N E S W

42

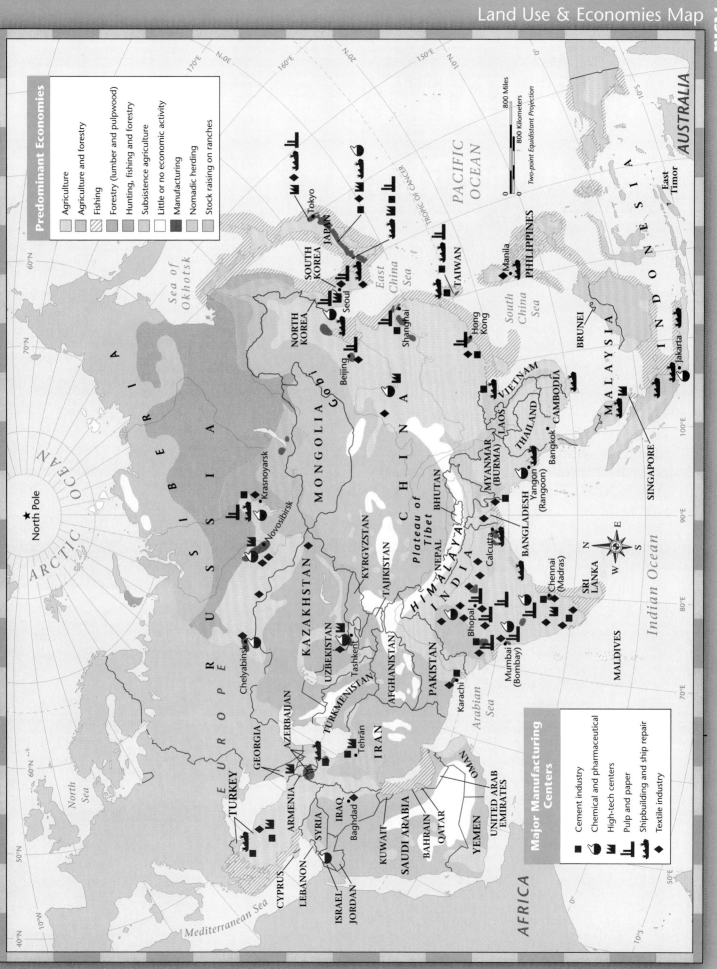

Predominant Economies

- Agriculture
- Agriculture and forestry
- Fishing
- Forestry (lumber and pulpwood)
- Hunting, fishing and forestry
- Subsistence agriculture
- Little or no economic activity
- Manufacturing
- Nomadic herding
- Stock raising on ranches

Major Manufacturing Centers

- Cement industry
- Chemical and pharmaceutical
- High-tech centers
- Pulp and paper
- Shipbuilding and ship repair
- Textile industry

43

Australia & Oceania

Sometimes called the "land down under," Australia dominates the southwestern Pacific Ocean, but it is not alone. Many islands are sprinkled across the deep waters of the Pacific. New Zealand and New Guinea are large compared with tiny island nations such as Tuvalu and Vanuatu. Islands of Oceania, as the Pacific region is sometimes called, range from forest-covered mountains to ring-shaped coral islands called atolls. The middle of Australia is very dry, so most people live in cities near the coast.

Sheep population in millions, 2002

Australia 136

New Zealand 45

Russia/Baltic States 61

China 136

Uruguay 20

Argentina 19

South Africa 31

UK 29

USA 7

Sheep Farming Nations

Australia and New Zealand have almost 24 million people. But humans are not the largest population in these two countries. There are over seven times more sheep than people!

Australia

▲ *Sydney Opera House, perched on the edge of the city's harbor, is a symbol of modern Australia.*

▶*Young men perform a traditional victory dance wearing costumes made of palm leaves, grass, and flowers.*

Fiji Islands

▲ The warm waters of the equatorial Pacific Ocean are rich in marine life, such as this large sea turtle.

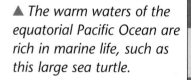

◄ Isolation has resulted in unique wildlife in Australia. This red kangaroo carries her baby–called a "joey"–in a pouch on her stomach.

Australia

45

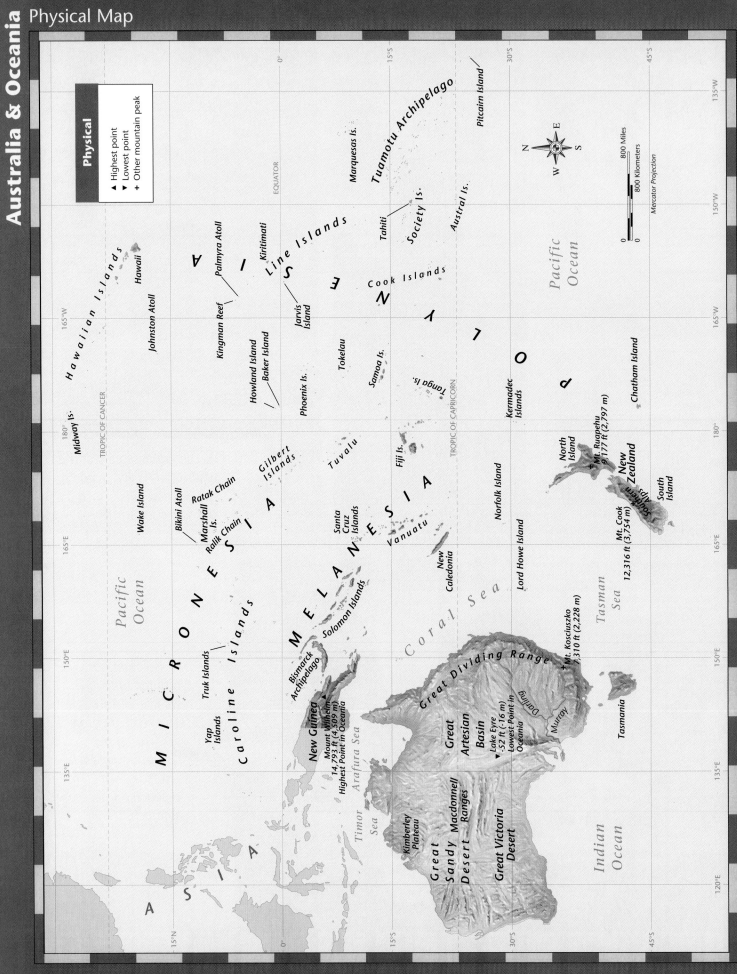

Physical

▲ Highest point
▼ Lowest point
+ Other mountain peak

Hawaiian Islands

Midway Is.

Johnston Atoll

Hawaii

Palmyra Atoll

Kingman Reef

Kiritimati

Jarvis Island

Line Islands

Marquesas Is.

Tuamotu Archipelago

Pitcairn Island

Tahiti

Society Is.

Austral Is.

EQUATOR

N E W

Howland Island

Baker Island

Phoenix Is.

Tokelau

Samoa Is.

Cook Islands

Pacific Ocean

Wake Island

Bikini Atoll

Ratak Chain

Marshall Is.

Ralik Chain

Gilbert Islands

Tuvalu

Fiji Is.

Tonga Is.

TROPIC OF CAPRICORN

Kermadec Islands

P O L Y N E S I A

M I C R O N E S I A

Pacific Ocean

Yap Islands

Truk Islands

Caroline Islands

M E L A N E S I A

Santa Cruz Islands

Vanuatu

New Caledonia

Norfolk Island

Lord Howe Island

North Island

Mt. Ruapehu 9,177 ft (2,797 m)

New Zealand

South Island

Southern Alps

Mt. Cook 12,316 ft (3,754 m)

Chatham Island

Tasman Sea

Coral Sea

Bismarck Archipelago

Solomon Islands

New Guinea

Mount Wilhelm ▲ 14,793 ft (4,509 m) Highest Point in Oceania

Arafura Sea

Timor Sea

A S I A

Great Dividing Range

Mt. Kosciuszko + 7,310 ft (2,228 m)

Great Artesian Basin

Lake Eyre ▼ -52 ft (-16 m) Lowest Point in Oceania

Darling

Murray

Tasmania

Kimberley Plateau

Great Sandy Desert

Macdonnell Ranges

Great Victoria Desert

Indian Ocean

800 Miles

800 Kilometers

Mercator Projection

TROPIC OF CANCER

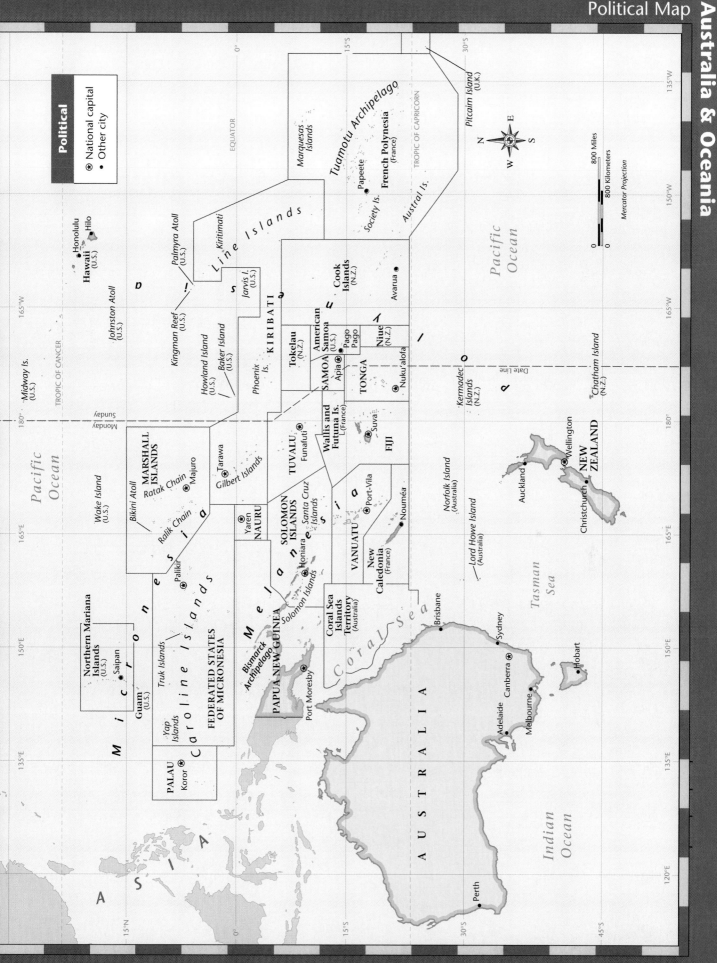

Political
⊛ National capital
• Other city

EQUATOR

0°

15°S

30°S

135°W

TROPIC OF CAPRICORN

Pitcairn Island
(U.K.)

N
W E
S

800 Miles
800 Kilometers
0   0
Mercator Projection

Tuamotu Archipelago

Marquesas
Islands

Papeete
French Polynesia
(France)

Society Is.

Austral Is.

Pacific
Ocean

150°W

Hawaii
(U.S.)
Honolulu
Hilo

Johnston Atoll
(U.S.)

TROPIC OF CANCER

165°W

P o l y n e s i a

Palmyra Atoll
(U.S.)

Line Islands

Kiritimati

Jarvis I.
(U.S.)

Kingman Reef
(U.S.)

Cook
Islands
(N.Z.)

Avarua

165°W

Chatham Island
(N.Z.)

Howland Island
(U.S.)

Baker Island
(U.S.)

KIRIBATI

Phoenix
Is.

Tokelau
(N.Z.)

American
Samoa
(U.S.)

Pago
Pago

Niue
(N.Z.)

Nuku'alofa

Date Line

Kermadec
Islands
(N.Z.)

180°

Midway Is.
(U.S.)

180°

Monday
Sunday

MARSHALL
ISLANDS

Ratak Chain

Majuro

Tarawa

Gilbert Islands

TUVALU

Funafuti

SAMOA
Apia

TONGA

Wallis and
Futuna Is.
(France)

Suva

FIJI

Wake Island
(U.S.)

Bikini Atoll

Ralik Chain

M i c r o n e s i a

Palikir

Nauru
NAURU
Yaren

SOLOMON
ISLANDS

Honiara

Santa Cruz
Islands

Solomon Islands

M e l a n e s i a

VANUATU

Port-Vila

Norfolk Island
(Australia)

New
Caledonia
(France)

Nouméa

Lord Howe Island
(Australia)

New
Zealand
Wellington

Auckland

Christchurch

NEW
ZEALAND

165°E

Tasman
Sea

Pacific
Ocean

165°E

15°N

Northern Mariana
Islands
(U.S.)

Saipan

Guam
(U.S.)

Truk Islands

Caroline Islands

FEDERATED STATES
OF MICRONESIA

Yap
Islands

PALAU
Koror

150°E

Bismarck
Archipelago

PAPUA NEW GUINEA

Port Moresby

Coral Sea
Islands Territory
(Australia)

Coral Sea

Brisbane

Sydney

Canberra

Melbourne

Hobart

Adelaide

A U S T R A L I A

Perth

135°E

A S I A

0°

120°E

Indian
Ocean

15°S

30°S

45°S

47

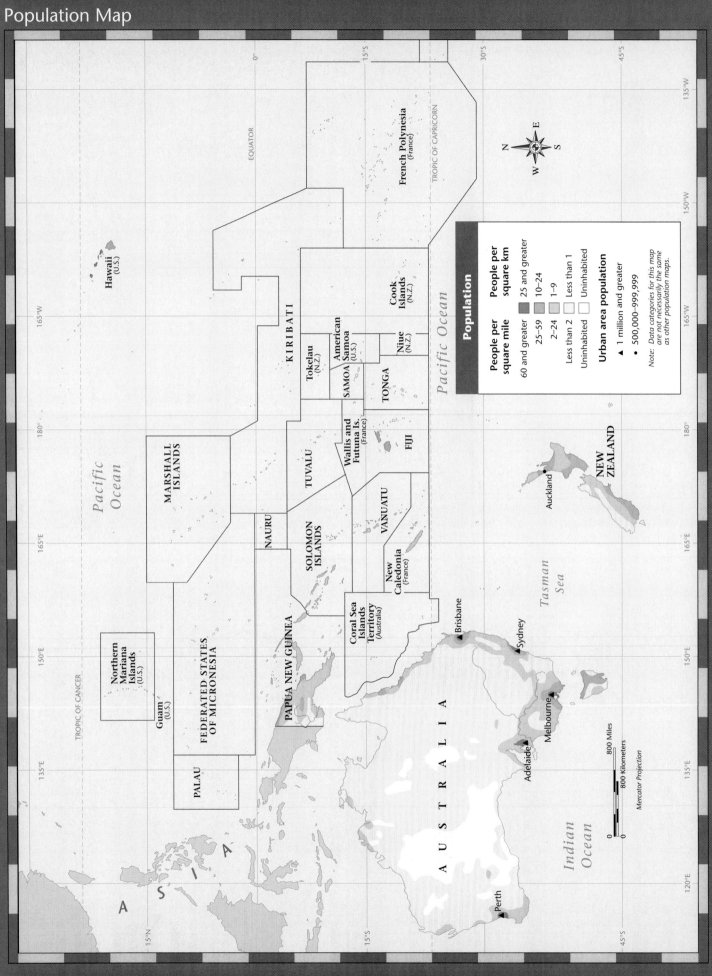

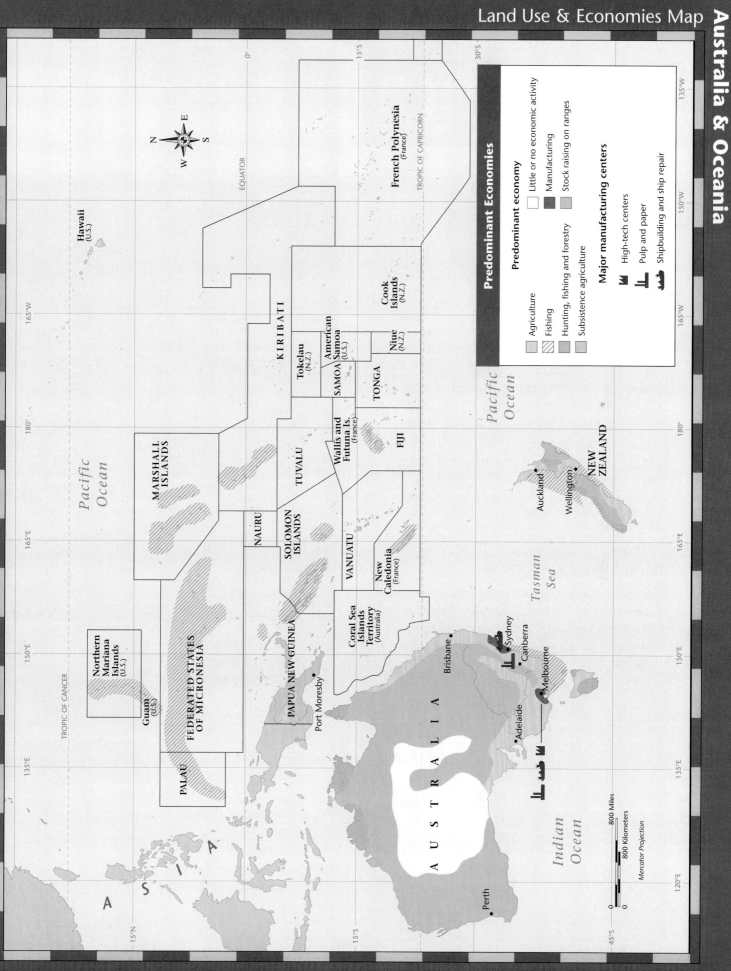

Predominant Economies

Predominant economy

- Agriculture
- Fishing
- Hunting, fishing and forestry
- Subsistence agriculture
- Little or no economic activity
- Manufacturing
- Stock raising on ranges

Major manufacturing centers

- High-tech centers
- Pulp and paper
- Shipbuilding and ship repair

Pacific Ocean

Hawaii (U.S.)

KIRIBATI

French Polynesia (France)

TROPIC OF CAPRICORN

EQUATOR

Cook Islands (N.Z.)

Tokelau (N.Z.)

American Samoa (U.S.)

SAMOA

Niue (N.Z.)

TONGA

Wallis and Futuna Is. (France)

FIJI

MARSHALL ISLANDS

TUVALU

Pacific Ocean

NAURU

SOLOMON ISLANDS

VANUATU

New Caledonia (France)

NEW ZEALAND

Auckland

Wellington

Tasman Sea

Northern Mariana Islands (U.S.)

Guam (U.S.)

FEDERATED STATES OF MICRONESIA

PALAU

PAPUA NEW GUINEA

Port Moresby

Coral Sea Islands Territory (Australia)

Brisbane

Sydney

Canberra

Melbourne

Adelaide

A U S T R A L I A

Perth

Indian Ocean

A S I A

TROPIC OF CANCER

800 Miles

800 Kilometers

Mercator Projection

TROPIC OF CANCER

Pacific Ocean

Antarctica

Graham Land

Most of Antarctica lies below layers of snow and ice, often over three miles thick. In addition to being the coldest of all the continents, Antarctica is different in many ways. It has no permanent population and no cities. Scientists live and work in research stations in this remote place for a few months at a time. Only a few species of animals, such as penguins and seals, have adapted to the bitter cold.

The Size of an Iceberg

Most icebergs—blocks of ice floating in the ocean—form along the coasts of Alaska, Greenland, and Antarctica. Icebergs may look small, but actually as much as 90% of an iceberg's mass may be below the surface of the water.

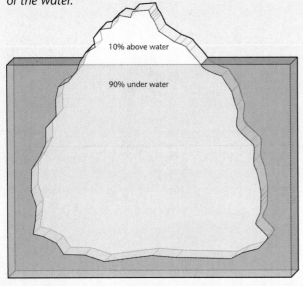

10% above water

90% under water

▲ *Sunlight turns the snow and ice of the Antarctic Peninsula shades of gold and rose.*

▶ *Scientists live in shelters at the South Pole. The United States and 23 other countries use Antarctica as a giant laboratory to study Earth.*

South Pole, Antarctica

▼ Elephant seals are one of the few mammals able to live in Antarctica's frigid environment.

Ross Ice Shelf

◀ Penguins catch fish in the icy waters that surround Antarctica.

WELCOMES YOU
SOUTH POLE

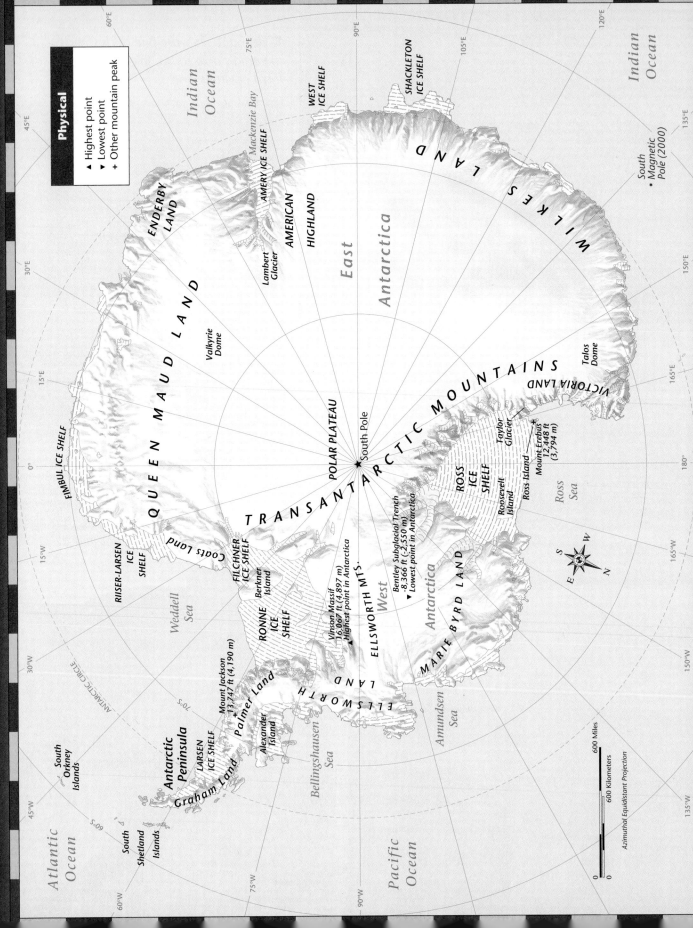

Physical

▲ Highest point
▼ Lowest point
+ Other mountain peak

Indian Ocean

Atlantic Ocean

Pacific Ocean

ENDERBY LAND

QUEEN MAUD LAND

WILKES LAND

East Antarctica

West Antarctica

TRANSANTARCTIC MOUNTAINS

POLAR PLATEAU

South Pole

VICTORIA LAND

MARIE BYRD LAND

ELLSWORTH LAND

Antarctic Peninsula

Graham Land

Palmer Land

Coats Land

AMERY ICE SHELF

AMERICAN HIGHLAND

WEST ICE SHELF

SHACKLETON ICE SHELF

FIMBUL ICE SHELF

RIISER-LARSEN ICE SHELF

FILCHNER ICE SHELF

RONNE ICE SHELF

ROSS ICE SHELF

LARSEN ICE SHELF

Lambert Glacier

Mackenzie Bay

Valkyrie Dome

Talos Dome

Taylor Glacier

Ross Island

Roosevelt Island

Berkner Island

Alexander Island

ELLSWORTH MTS.

Vinson Massif
16,067 ft (4,897 m)
▲ Highest point in Antarctica

Bentley Subglacial Trench
-8,366 ft (-2,550 m)
▼ Lowest point in Antarctica

Mount Erebus
12,448 ft
(3,794 m)

Mount Jackson
13,747 ft (4,190 m)

South Magnetic Pole (2000)

South Orkney Islands

South Shetland Islands

Weddell Sea

Ross Sea

Bellingshausen Sea

Amundsen Sea

ANTARCTIC CIRCLE

60°E
75°E
90°E
105°E
120°E
135°E
150°E
165°E
180°
165°W
150°W
135°W
90°W
75°W
60°W
45°W
30°W
15°W
0°
15°E
30°E
45°E

60°S
70°S

N W S E

0   600 Miles
0   600 Kilometers

Azimuthal Equidistant Projection

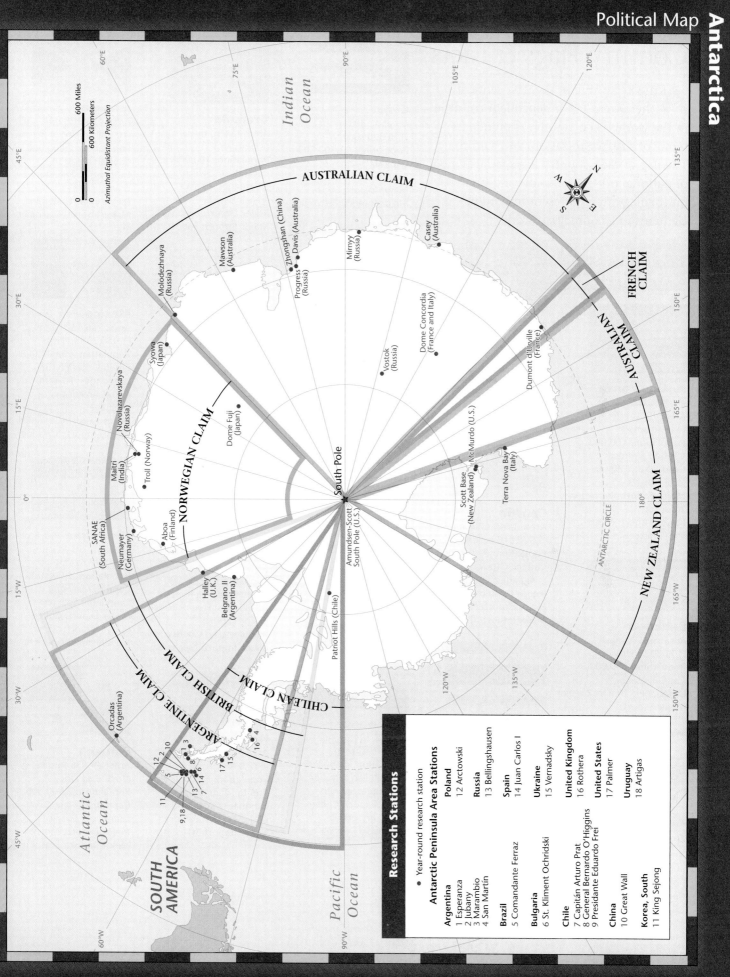

Political Map

Antarctica

Indian Ocean

600 Miles
600 Kilometers
Azimuthal Equidistant Projection

AUSTRALIAN CLAIM

FRENCH CLAIM

AUSTRALIAN CLAIM

NEW ZEALAND CLAIM

NORWEGIAN CLAIM

BRITISH CLAIM

ARGENTINE CLAIM

CHILEAN CLAIM

South Pole

Molodezhnaya (Russia)
Mawson (Australia)
Zhongshan (China)
Davis (Australia)
Progress (Russia)
Mirnyy (Russia)
Casey (Australia)
Dome Concordia (France and Italy)
Vostok (Russia)
Syowa (Japan)
Novolazarevskaya (Russia)
Dome Fuji (Japan)
Dumont d'Urville (France)
Maitri (India)
Troll (Norway)
McMurdo (U.S.)
Terra Nova Bay (Italy)
SANAE (South Africa)
Aboa (Finland)
Scott Base (New Zealand)
Neumayer (Germany)
Amundsen-Scott South Pole (U.S.)
Halley (U.K.)
Belgrano II (Argentina)
Patriot Hills (Chile)
Orcadas (Argentina)
12 2 10
1 3
16 4
5 8
13 6
7 14
17
15
9,18
11

Atlantic Ocean

Pacific Ocean

SOUTH AMERICA

ANTARCTIC CIRCLE

60°E
75°E
90°E
105°E
120°E
135°E
150°E
165°E
180°
165°W
150°W
135°W
120°W
90°W
60°W
45°W
30°W
15°W
0°
15°E
30°E
45°E

Research Stations

• Year-round research station

Antarctic Peninsula Area Stations

Argentina
1 Esperanza
2 Jubany
3 Marambio
4 San Martín

Brazil
5 Comandante Ferraz

Bulgaria
6 St. Kliment Ochridski

Chile
7 Capitán Arturo Prat
8 General Bernardo O'Higgins
9 Presidante Eduardo Frei

China
10 Great Wall

Korea, South
11 King Sejong

Poland
12 Arctowski

Russia
13 Bellingshausen

Spain
14 Juan Carlos I

Ukraine
15 Vernadsky

United Kingdom
16 Rothera

United States
17 Palmer

Uruguay
18 Artigas

Country Flags & Facts

At the beginning of the 21st century there were 191 independent countries in the world. Each country is unique in terms of size, organization, and culture. The flag of each country is a special symbol of national pride. The colors and symbols on the flag often represent important elements of a country's history.

NORTH AMERICA

Antigua and Barbuda
Area: 170 sq mi (440 sq km)
Population: 100,000
Capital: St. John's
Languages: English, local dialects
Major Export: Petroleum Products
Major Import: Foods and Livestock

Bahamas
Area: 5,359 sq mi (13,880 sq km)
Population: 300,000
Capital: Nassau
Languages: English, Creole
Major Export: Pharmaceuticals
Major Import: Foods

Barbados
Area: 166 sq mi (430 sq km)
Population: 300,000
Capital: Bridgetown
Language: English
Major Export: Sugar
Major Import: Manufactured Goods

Belize
Area: 8,865 sq mi (22,960 sq km)
Population: 300,000
Capital: Belmopan
Language: English
Major Export: Sugar
Major Import: Machinery

Canada
Area: 3,849,670 sq mi (9,970,610 sq km)
Population: 31,000,000
Capital: Ottawa
Languages: English, French (both official)
Major Export: Newsprint
Major Import: Crude Oil

Costa Rica
Area: 19,730 sq mi (51,100 sq km)
Population: 3,700,000
Capital: San José
Language: Spanish
Major Export: Coffee
Major Import: Raw Materials

Cuba
Area: 42,803 sq mi (110,860 sq km)
Population: 11,300,000
Capital: Havana
Language: Spanish
Major Export: Sugar
Major Import: Petroleum

Dominica
Area: 290 sq mi (751 sq km)
Population: 100,000
Capital: Roseau
Languages: English, French
Major Export: Bananas
Major Import: Manufactured Goods

Dominican Republic
Area: 18,815 sq mi (48,731 sq km)
Population: 8,600,000
Capital: Santo Domingo
Language: Spanish
Major Export: Ferronickel
Major Import: Foods

El Salvador
Area: 8,124 sq mi (21,041 sq km)
Population: 6,400,000
Capital: San Salvador
Language: Spanish
Major Export: Coffee
Major Import: Raw Materials

Grenada
Area: 131 sq mi (339 sq km)
Population: 100,000
Capital: St. George's
Languages: English, French patois
Major Export: Bananas
Major Import: Foods

Guatemala
Area: 42,042 sq mi (108,889 sq km)
Population: 13,000,000
Capital: Guatemala City
Languages: Spanish, Mayan dialects
Major Export: Coffee
Major Import: Petroleum

Haiti
Area: 10,714 sq mi (27,750 sq km)
Population: 7,000,000
Capital: Port-au-Prince
Languages: French, Creole
Major Export: Manufactured Goods
Major Import: Machinery

Honduras
Area: 43,278 sq mi (112,090 sq km)
Population: 6,700,000
Capital: Tegucigalpa
Language: Spanish
Major Export: Bananas
Major Import: Machinery

Jamaica
Area: 4,243 sq mi (10,989 sq km)
Population: 2,600,000
Capital: Kingston
Languages: English, Creole
Major Export: Alumina
Major Import: Machinery

Mexico
Area: 756,062 sq mi (1,958,201 sq km)
Population: 99,600,000
Capital: Mexico City
Languages: Spanish, Native American languages
Major Export: Crude Oil
Major Import: Machinery

Nicaragua
Area: 50,193 sq mi (129,999 sq km)
Population: 5,200,000
Capital: Managua
Language: Spanish
Major Export: Coffee
Major Import: Manufactured Goods

Panama
Area: 29,158 sq mi (75,519 sq km)
Population: 2,900,000
Capital: Panama City
Language: Spanish
Major Export: Bananas
Major Import: Machinery

St. Kitts and Nevis
Area: 139 sq mi
(360 sq km)
Population: 40,000
Capital: Basseterre
Language: English
Major Export: Machinery
Major Import:
Electronic Goods

St. Lucia
Area: 239 sq mi
(619 sq km)
Population: 200,000
Capital: Castries
Languages: English,
French patois
Major Export: Bananas
Major Import: Foods

St. Vincent and
the Grenadines
Area: 151 sq mi
(391 sq km)
Population: 100,000
Capital: Kingstown
Languages: English,
French
Major Export: Bananas
Major Import: Foods

Trinidad and
Tobago
Area: 1,981 sq mi
(5,131 sq km)
Population: 1,300,000
Capital: Port-of-Spain
Language: English
Major Export: Petroleum
Major Import: Machinery

United States
Area: 3,717,796 sq mi
(9,629,091 sq km)
Population: 284,500,000
Capital: Washington, D.C.
Language: English
Major Export: Machinery
Major Import: Crude Oil

SOUTH AMERICA

Argentina
Area: 1,073,514 sq mi
(2,780,401 sq km)
Population: 37,500,000
Capital: Buenos Aires
Language: Spanish
Major Export: Meat
Major Import: Machinery

Bolivia
Area: 424,162 sq mi
(1,098,580 sq km)
Population: 8,500,000
Capitals: La Paz, Sucre
Languages: Spanish,
Quechua, Aymara (all official)
Major Export: Metals
Major Import: Machinery

Brazil
Area: 3,300,154 sq mi
(8,547,399 sq km)
Population: 171,800,000
Capital: Brasília
Language: Portuguese
Major Export: Iron Ore
Major Import: Crude Oil

Chile
Area: 292,135 sq mi
(756,626 sq km)
Population: 15,400,000
Capital: Santiago
Language: Spanish
Major Export: Copper
Major Import: Machinery

Colombia
Area: 439,734 sq mi
(1,138,511 sq km)
Population: 43,100,000
Capital: Bogotá
Language: Spanish
Major Export: Petroleum
Major Import: Machinery

Ecuador
Area: 109,483 sq mi
(283,561 sq km)
Population: 12,900,000
Capital: Quito
Languages: Spanish,
Quechua
Major Export: Petroleum
Major Import: Transport
Equipment

Guyana
Area: 83,000 sq mi
(214,969 sq km)
Population: 700,000
Capital: Georgetown
Language: English
Major Export: Sugar
Major Import:
Manufactured Goods

Paraguay
Area: 157,046 sq mi
(406,749 sq km)
Population: 5,700,000
Capital: Asunción
Languages: Spanish, Guaraní
Major Export: Cotton
Major Import: Machinery

Peru
Area: 496,224 sq mi
(1,285,220 sq km)
Population: 26,100,000
Capital: Lima
Languages: Spanish,
Quechua (both official),
Aymara
Major Export: Copper
Major Import: Machinery

Suriname
Area: 63,039 sq mi
(163,271 sq km)
Population: 400,000
Capital: Paramaribo
Languages: Dutch
Major Export: Bauxite
Major Import: Machinery

Uruguay
Area: 68,498 sq mi
(177,410 sq km)
Population: 3,400,000
Capital: Montevideo
Languages: Spanish
Major Export: Wool
Major Import: Machinery

Venezuela
Area: 352,143 sq mi
(912,050 sq km)
Population: 24,600,000
Capital: Caracas
Language: Spanish
Major Export: Petroleum
Major Import:
Raw Materials

AFRICA

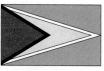

Algeria
Area: 919,591 sq mi
(2,381,521 sq km)
Population: 31,000,000
Capital: Algiers
Languages: Arabic, French,
Berber
Major Export: Petroleum
Major Import: Machinery

Angola
Area: 481,351 sq mi
(1,246,699 sq km)
Population: 12,300,000
Capital: Luanda
Languages: Portuguese,
local languages
Major Export: Crude Oil
Major Import: Machinery

Benin
Area: 43,483 sq mi
(112,621 sq km)
Population: 6,600,000
Capital: Porto-Novo
Languages: French, Fon,
Yoruba
Major Export: Cotton
Major Import: Foods

Botswana
Area: 224,606 sq mi
(581,730 sq km)
Population: 1,600,000
Capital: Gaborone
Languages: English, Setswana
Major Export: Diamonds
Major Import: Foods

Burkina Faso
Area: 105,792 sq mi
(274,000 sq km)
Population: 12,300,000
Capital: Ouagadougou
Languages: French, local languages
Major Export: Cotton
Major Import: Machinery

Burundi
Area: 10,745 sq mi
(27,830 sq km)
Population: 6,200,000
Capital: Bujumbura
Languages: Kirundi,
French (both official)
Major Export: Coffee
Major Import: Machinery

Cameroon
Area: 183,568 sq mi
(475,442 sq km)
Population: 15,800,000
Capital: Yaoundé
Languages: French, English
local languages
Major Export: Crude Oil
Major Import: Machinery

Cape Verde
Area: 1,556 sq mi
(4,030 sq km)
Population: 400,000
Capital: Praia
Languages: Portuguese,
Crioulo
Major Export: Shoes
Major Import: Foods

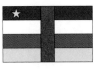

Central African Republic
Area: 240,533 sq mi
(622,980 sq km)
Population: 3,600,000
Capital: Bangui
Languages: French,
Sango, Arabic, Hunsa
Major Export: Diamonds
Major Import: Foods

Chad
Area: 495,753 sq mi
(1,283,948 sq km)
Population: 8,700,000
Capital: N'Djamena
Languages: French, Arabic
(both official), Sara, Sango,
Major Export: Cotton
Major Import: Machinery

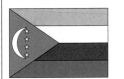

Comoros
Area: 861 sq mi
(2,230 sq km)
Population: 600,000
Capital: Moroni
Languages: Arabic, French
(both official), Comoran
Major Export: Vanilla
Major Import: Rice

Congo
Area: 132,046 sq mi
(341,999 sq km)
Population: 3,100,000
Capital: Brazzaville
Languages: French,
Lingala, Monokutuba
Major Export: Crude Oil
Major Import: Machinery

Congo, Democratic Republic of the
Area: 905,351 sq mi
(2,344,859 sq km)
Population: 53,600,000
Capital: Kinshasa
Languages: French,
Lingala, Kingwana
Major Export: Diamonds
Major Import:
Manufactured Goods

Côte d'Ivoire
Area: 124,502 sq mi
(322,460 sq km)
Population: 16,400,000
Capitals: Yamoussoukro,
Abidjan
Languages: French,
Dioula
Major Export: Cocoa
Major Import: Foods

Djibouti
Area: 8,958 sq mi
(23,200 sq km)
Population: 600,000
Capital: Djibouti
Languages: French, Arabic
(both official)
Major Export: Hides
and Skins
Major Import: Foods

Egypt
Area: 386,660 sq mi
(1,001,449 sq km)
Population: 69,800,000
Capital: Cairo
Language: Arabic
Major Export: Crude Oil
Major Import: Machinery

Equatorial Guinea
Area: 10,830 sq mi
(28,050 sq km)
Population: 500,000
Capital: Malabo
Languages: Spanish,
French (both official),
Fang, Bubi, Ibo
Major Export: Petroleum
Major Import: Machinery

Eritrea
Area: 45,405 sq mi
(117,599 sq km)
Population: 4,300,000
Capital: Asmara
Languages: Afar, Amharic,
Arabic, Tigre
Major Export: Livestock
Major Import: Processed
Foods

Ethiopia
Area: 426,371 sq mi
(1,104,301 sq km)
Population: 65,400,000
Capital: Addis Ababa
Languages: Amharic,
Tigrinya, Orominga
Major Export: Coffee
Major Import: Foods
and Livestock

Gabon
Area: 103,347 sq mi
(267,667 sq km)
Population: 1,200,000
Capital: Libreville
Languages: French, local
languages
Major Export: Crude Oil
Major Import: Machinery

Gambia
Area: 4,363 sq mi
(11,300 sq km)
Population: 1,400,000
Capital: Banjul
Languages: English,
Mandinka, Fula
Major Export: Peanuts
Major Import: Foods

Ghana
Area: 92,100 sq mi
(238,537 sq km)
Population: 19,900,000
Capital: Accra
Languages: English,
local languages
Major Export: Gold
Major Import: Machinery

Guinea
Area: 94,927 sq mi
(245,861 sq km)
Population: 7,600,000
Capital: Conakry
Languages: French,
local languages
Major Export: Bauxite
Major Import: Petroleum
Products

Guinea-Bissau
Area: 13,946 sq mi
(36,120 sq km)
Population: 1,200,000
Capital: Bissau
Languages: Portuguese,
Crioulo, Fula
Major Export: Cashews
Major Import: Foods

Kenya
Area: 224,081 sq mi
(580,370 sq km)
Population: 29,800,000
Capital: Nairobi
Languages: English,
Swahili (both official)
Major Export: Tea
Major Import: Machinery

Lesotho
Area: 11,718 sq mi
(30,350 sq km)
Population: 2,200,000
Capital: Maseru
Languages: English,
Sesotho, Zulu, Xhosa
Major Export: Clothing
Major Import: Corn

Liberia
Area: 43,000 sq mi
(111,369 sq km)
Population: 3,200,000
Capital: Monrovia
Languages: English, local
languages
Major Export: Diamonds
Major Import: Natural Gas

Libya
Area: 679,359 sq mi
(1,759,540 sq km)
Population: 5,200,000
Capital: Tripoli
Language: Arabic
Major Export: Crude Oil
Major Import: Machinery

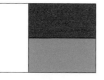

Madagascar
Area: 226,656 sq mi
(587,039 sq km)
Population: 16,400,000
Capital: Antananarivo
Languages: French,
Malagasy (both official)
Major Export: Coffee
Major Import: Machinery

Malawi
Area: 45,745 sq mi
(118,480 sq km)
Population: 10,500,000
Capital: Lilongwe
Languages: Chewa,
English (both official)
Major Export: Tobacco
Major Import: Foods

Mali
Area: 478,838 sq mi
(1,240,307 sq km)
Population: 11,000,000
Capital: Bamako
Languages: French,
Bambara
Major Export: Cotton
Major Import: Machinery

Mauritania
Area: 395,954 sq mi
(1,025,521 sq km)
Population: 2,700,000
Capital: Nouakchott
Languages: Hasaniya
Arabic, Wolof (both official)
Major Export: Fish
Major Import: Foods

Mauritius
Area: 788 sq mi
(2,040 sq km)
Population: 1,200,000
Capital: Port Louis
Languages: English,
Creole, French, Bhojpuri
Major Export: Sugar
Major Import: Foods

Morocco
Area: 279,757 sq mi
(724,571 sq km)
Population: 29,500,000
Capital: Rabat
Languages: Arabic,
Berber, French
Major Export: Foods
Major Import:
Manufactured Goods

Mozambique
Area: 309,494 sq mi
(801,598 sq km)
Population: 19,400,000
Capital: Maputo
Languages: Portuguese,
local languages
Major Export: Cashews
Major Import: Foods

Namibia
Area: 318,259 sq mi
(824,291 sq km)
Population: 1,800,000
Capital: Windhoek
Languages: English,
Afrikaans, local languages
Major Export: Diamonds
Major Import:
Construction Materials

Niger
Area: 489,189 sq mi
(1,267,000 sq km)
Population: 10,400,000
Capital: Niamey
Languages: French, Hausa,
Djerma
Major Export: Uranium
Major Import:
Manufactured Goods

Nigeria
Area: 356,668 sq mi
(923,770 sq km)
Population: 126,600,000
Capital: Abuja
Languages: English,
Hausa, Yoruba, Igbo
Major Export: Petroleum
Major Import: Machinery

Rwanda
Area: 10,170 sq mi
(26,340 sq km)
Population: 7,300,000
Capital: Kigali
Languages: Kinyarwanda,
French, English (all official)
Major Export: Coffee
Major Import: Foods

Sao Tome and
Principe
Area: 371 sq mi
(961 sq km)
Population: 260,000
Capital: São Tomé
Language: Portuguese,
Criulo
Major Export: Cocoa
Major Import: Textiles

Senegal
Area: 75,954 sq mi
(196,721 sq km)
Population: 9,700,000
Capital: Dakar
Languages: French, Wolof,
Pulaar, Diola
Major Export: Fish
Major Import: Foods

Seychelles
Area: 174 sq mi
(451 sq km)
Population: 100,000
Capital: Victoria
Languages: English, French
(both official), Creole
Major Export: Fish
Major Import: Foods

Sierra Leone
Area: 27,699 sq mi
(71,740 sq km)
Population: 5,400,000
Capital: Freetown
Languages: English,
Mende, Temne, Krio
Major Export: Diamonds
Major Import: Foods

Somalia
Area: 246,201 sq mi
(637,657 sq km)
Population: 7,500,000
Capital: Mogadishu
Languages: Somali, Arabic,
Major Export: Livestock
Major Import: Textiles

South Africa
Area: 471,444 sq mi
(1,221,038 sq km)
Population: 43,600,000
Capitals: Pretoria, Cape
Town, Bloemfontein
Languages: Afrikaans,
English, Zulu (all official)
Major Export: Gold
Major Import: Transport
Equipment

Sudan
Area: 967,494 sq mi
(2,505,809 sq km)
Population: 31,800,000
Capital: Khartoum
Languages: Arabic,
Nubian, Ta Bedawie
Major Export: Cotton
Major Import: Petroleum
Products

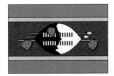

Swaziland
Area: 6,703 sq mi
(17,361 sq km)
Population: 1,100,000
Capital: Mbabane
Languages: English, Swazi
(both official)
Major Export: Soft Drink
Concentrates
Major Import: Machinery

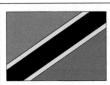

Tanzania
Area: 364,900 sq mi
(945,087 sq km)
Population: 36,200,000
Capitals: Dar es Salaam,
Dodoma
Languages: Swahili, English
(both official)
Major Export: Coffee
Major Import: Machinery

Togo
Area: 21,927 sq mi
(56,791 sq km)
Population: 5,200,000
Capital: Lomé
Languages: French, Ewe,
Mina, Kabye
Major Export:
Phosphates
Major Import:
Manufactured Goods

Tunisia
Area: 63,170 sq mi
(163,610 sq km)
Population: 9,700,000
Capital: Tunis
Languages: Arabic, French
Major Export: Petroleum
Products
Major Import: Machinery

Uganda
Area: 93,066 sq mi
(241,041 sq km)
Population: 24,000,000
Capital: Kampala
Languages: English, Ganda
Major Export: Coffee
Major Import: Machinery

Zambia
Area: 290,583 sq mi
(752,610 sq km)
Population: 9,800,000
Capital: Lusaka
Languages: English, local
languages
Major Export: Copper
Major Import:
Manufactured Goods

Zimbabwe
Area: 150,873 sq mi
(390,761 sq km)
Population: 11,400,000
Capital: Harare
Languages: English,
Shona, Sindebele
Major Export: Gold
Major Import: Machinery

EUROPE

Albania
Area: 11,100 sq mi
(28,748 sq km)
Population: 3,400,000
Capital: Tirana
Language: Albanian
Major Export: Asphalt
Major Import: Machinery

Andorra
Area: 174 sq mi
(451 sq km)
Population: 100,000
Capital: Andorra la Vella
Languages: Catalan,
French, Spanish
Major Export: Electricity
Major Import:
Manufactured Goods

Austria
Area: 32,378 sq mi
(83,859 sq km)
Population: 8,100,000
Capital: Vienna
Language: German
Major Export: Machinery
Major Import: Petroleum

Belarus
Area: 80,154 sq mi
(207,598 sq km)
Population: 10,000,000
Capital: Minsk
Languages: Belarussian,
Russian
Major Export: Machinery
Major Import: Fuels

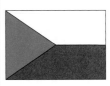

Belgium
Area: 11,787 sq mi
(30,528 sq km)
Population: 10,300,000
Capital: Brussels
Languages: Flemish,
French
Major Export: Iron and
Steel
Major Import: Fuels

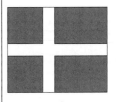

Bosnia and
Herzegovina
Area: 19,741 sq mi
(51,129 sq km)
Population: 3,400,000
Capital: Sarajevo
Language: Serbo-Croatian
Major Export: N/A
Major Import: N/A

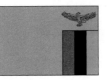

Bulgaria
Area: 42,822 sq mi
(110,909 sq km)
Population: 8,100,000
Capital: Sofia
Language: Bulgarian
Major Export: Machinery
Major Import: Fuels

Croatia
Area: 21,830 sq mi
(56,540 sq km)
Population: 4,700,000
Capital: Zagreb
Language: Serbo-Croatian
Major Export: Transport
Equipment
Major Import: Machinery

Czech Republic
Area: 30,448 sq mi
(78,860 sq km)
Population: 10,300,000
Capital: Prague
Languages: Czech, Slovak
Major Export: Machinery
Major Import: Crude Oil

Denmark
Area: 16,637 sq mi
(43,090 sq km)
Population: 5,400,000
Capital: Copenhagen
Language: Danish
Major Export: Machinery
Major Import: Machinery

Estonia
Area: 17,413 sq mi
(45,099 sq km)
Population: 1,400,000
Capital: Tallinn
Language: Estonian
Major Export: Textiles
Major Import: Machinery

Finland
Area: 130,560 sq mi
(338,150 sq km)
Population: 5,200,000
Capital: Helsinki
Languages: Finnish,
Swedish (both official)
Major Export: Paper
Major Import: Foods

France
Area: 212,934 sq mi
(551,499 sq km)
Population: 59,200,000
Capital: Paris
Language: French
Major Export: Machinery
Major Import: Crude Oil

Germany
Area: 137,830 sq mi
(356,978 sq km)
Population: 82,200,000
Capital: Berlin
Language: German
Major Export: Machinery
Major Import: Machinery

Greece
Area: 50,950 sq mi
(131,960 sq km)
Population: 10,900,000
Capital: Athens
Language: Greek
Major Export: Foods
Major Import: Machinery

Hungary
Area: 35,919 sq mi
(93,030 sq km)
Population: 10,000,000
Capital: Budapest
Language: Hungarian
Major Export: Machinery
Major Import: Crude Oil

Iceland
Area: 39,768 sq mi
(102,999 sq km)
Population: 300,000
Capital: Reykjavík
Language: Icelandic
Major Export: Fish
Major Import: Machinery

Ireland
Area: 27,135 sq mi
(70,280 sq km)
Population: 3,800,000
Capital: Dublin
Languages: English, Irish
Gaelic
Major Export: Chemicals
Major Import: Foods

Italy
Area: 116,320 sq mi
(301,269 sq km)
Population: 57,800,000
Capital: Rome
Language: Italian
Major Export: Metals
Major Import: Machinery

Latvia
Area: 24,942 sq mi
(64,599 sq km)
Population: 2,400,000
Capital: Ríga
Languages: Latvian,
Russian
Major Export: Wood
Major Import: Fuels

Liechtenstein
Area: 62 sq mi
(160 sq km)
Population: 30,000
Capital: Vaduz
Language: German
Major Export: Machinery
Major Import: Machinery

Lithuania
Area: 25,174 sq mi
(65,200 sq km)
Population: 3,700,000
Capital: Vilnius
Languages: Lithuanian,
Polish, Russian
Major Export: Foods and
Livestock
Major Import: Minerals

Luxembourg
Area: 999 sq mi
(2,587 sq km)
Population: 400,000
Capital: Luxembourg
Languages:
Luxembourgian,
German, French
Major Export:
Steel Products
Major Import: Minerals

Macedonia
Area: 9,927 sq mi
(25,711 sq km)
Population: 2,000,000
Capital: Skopje
Languages: Macedonian,
Albanian
Major Export:
Manufactured Goods
Major Import: Fuels

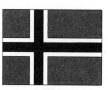

Malta
Area: 124 sq mi
(321 sq km)
Population: 400,000
Capital: Valletta
Languages: Maltese,
English (both official)
Major Export: Machinery
Major Import: Foods

Moldova
Area: 13,012 sq mi
(33,701 sq km)
Population: 4,300,000
Capital: Chişinău
Languages: Moldovan,
Russian
Major Export: Foods
Major Import: Petroleum

Monaco
Area: 1 sq mi
(2.6 sq km)
Population: 30,000
Capital: Monaco
Languages: French
Major Export: N/A
Major Import: N/A

Netherlands
Area: 15,768 sq mi
(40,839 sq km)
Population: 16,000,000
Capital: Amsterdam
Language: Dutch
Major Export:
Manufactured Goods
Major Import: Raw
Materials

Norway
Area: 125,050 sq mi
(323,880 sq km)
Population: 4,500,000
Capital: Oslo
Language: Norwegian
Major Export: Petroleum
Major Import: Machinery

Poland
Area: 124,807 sq mi
(323,250 sq km)
Population: 38,600,000
Capital: Warsaw
Language: Polish
Major Export:
Manufactured Goods
Major Import: Machinery

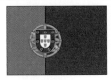

Portugal
Area: 35,514 sq mi
(91,981 sq km)
Population: 10,000,000
Capital: Lisbon
Language: Portuguese
Major Export: Clothing
Major Import: Machinery

Romania
Area: 92,042 sq mi
(238,389 sq km)
Population: 22,400,000
Capital: Bucharest
Languages: Romanian,
Hungarian
Major Export: Textiles
Major Import: Fuels

Russia
Area: 6,592,819 sq mi
(17,075,401 sq km)
Population: 144,400,000
Capital: Moscow
Languages: Russian, local
languages
Major Export: Petroleum
Major Import: Machinery

San Marino
Area: 23 sq mi
(60 sq km)
Population: 30,000
Capital: San Marino
Language: Italian
Major Export: Building
Stone
Major Import:
Manufactured Goods

Slovakia
Area: 18,923 sq mi
(49,011 sq km)
Population: 5,400,000
Capital: Bratislava
Languages: Slovak,
Hungarian
Major Export: Transport
Equipment
Major Import: Machinery

Slovenia
Area: 7,819 sq mi
(20,251 sq km)
Population: 2,000,000
Capital: Ljubljana
Languages: Slovene,
Serbo-Croatian
Major Export: Transport
Equipment
Major Import: Machinery

Spain
Area: 195,363 sq mi
(505,990 sq km)
Population: 39,800,000
Capital: Madrid
Languages: Spanish,
Catalan, Galician, Basque
Major Export: Cars and
Trucks
Major Import: Machinery

Sweden
Area: 173,730 sq mi
(449,961 sq km)
Population: 8,900,000
Capital: Stockholm
Language: Swedish
Major Export: Paper
Products
Major Import: Crude Oil

Switzerland
Area: 15,942 sq mi
(41,290 sq km)
Population: 7,200,000
Capital: Bern
Languages: German,
French, Italian
Major Export: Precision
Instruments
Major Import: Machinery

Ukraine
Area: 233,089 sq mi
(603,701 sq km)
Population: 49,100,000
Capital: Kiev
Languages: Ukrainian,
Russian
Major Export: Metals
Major Import: Machinery

United Kingdom
Area: 94,548 sq mi
(244,879 sq km)
Population: 60,000,000
Capital: London
Languages: English, Welsh,
Scottish Gaelic
Major Export:
Manufactured Goods
Major Import: Foods

Vatican City
Area: 0.2 sq mi
(0.4 sq km)
Population: 1,000
Languages: Italian, Latin
Major Export: N/A
Major Import: N/A

Yugoslavia
Area: 39,448 sq mi
(102,170 sq km)
Population: 10,700,000
Capital: Belgrade
Languages: Serbo-
Croatian, Albanian
Major Export:
Manufactured Goods
Major Import: Machinery

ASIA

Afghanistan
Area: 251,772 sq mi
(652,089 sq km)
Population: 26,800,000
Capital: Kabul
Languages: Pashto, Dari
Major Export: Fruits and
Nuts
Major Import: Foods

Armenia
Area: 11,506 sq mi
(29,801 sq km)
Population: 3,800,000
Capital: Yerevan
Languages: Armenian,
Russian
Major Export: Gold
Major Import: Grain

Azerbaijan
Area: 33,436 sq mi
(86,599 sq km)
Population: 8,100,000
Capital: Baku
Languages: Azeri, Russian,
Armenian
Major Export: Petroleum
Major Import: Machinery

Bahrain
Area: 266 sq mi
(689 sq km)
Population: 700,000
Capital: Manama
Language: Arabic
Major Export: Petroleum
Major Import: Machinery

Bangladesh
Area: 55,598 sq mi
(143,998 sq km)
Population: 133,500,000
Capital: Dhaka
Language: Bengali
Major Export: Clothing
Major Import: Machinery

Bhutan
Area: 18,147 sq mi
(47,001 sq km)
Population: 900,000
Capital: Thimphu
Languages: Dzonkha,
Local languages
Major Export: Cardamom
Major Import: Fuels

Brunei
Area: 2,228 sq mi
(5,771 sq km)
Population: 300,000
Capital: Bandar Seri
Begawan
Languages: Malay, English,
Chinese
Major Export: Crude Oil
Major Import: Machinery

Cambodia
Area: 69,900 sq mi
(181,041 sq km)
Population: 13,100,000
Capital: Phnom Penh
Languages: Khmer, French
Major Export: Timber
Major Import:
Construction Materials

China
Area: 3,696,100 sq mi
(9,572,899 sq km)
Population:
1,273,300,000
Capital: Beijing
Languages: Chinese,
Mandarin
Major Export: Machinery
Major Import: Machinery

Cyprus
Area: 3,571 sq mi
(9,249 sq km)
Population: 900,000
Capital: Nicosia
Languages: Greek, Turkish
Major Export: Citrus Fruits
Major Import:
Manufactured Goods

Georgia
Area: 26,911 sq mi
(69,699 sq km)
Population: 5,500,000
Capital: T'bilisi
Languages: Georgian,
Russian
Major Export: Citrus Fruits
Major Import: Fuels

India
Area: 1,269,340 sq mi
(3,287,606 sq km)
Population: 1,033,000,000
Capital: New Delhi
Languages: Hindi, English,
Local Languages
Major Export: Gems and
Jewelry
Major Import: Crude Oil

Indonesia
Area: 735,355 sq mi
(1,904,569 sq km)
Population: 206,100,000
Capital: Jakarta
Languages: Bahasa
Indonesia, Javanese
Major Export: Crude Oil
Major Import:
Manufactured Goods

Iran
Area: 630,575 sq mi
(1,633,189 sq km)
Population: 66,100,000
Capital: Tehran
Languages: Persian,
Kurdish
Major Export: Petroleum
Major Import: Machinery

Iraq
Area: 169,236 sq mi
(438,321 sq km)
Population: 23,600,000
Capital: Baghdad
Languages: Arabic,
Kurdish
Major Export: Crude Oil
Major Import: Machinery

Israel
Area: 8,131 sq mi
(21,059 sq km)
Population: 6,400,000
Capital: Jerusalem
Languages: Hebrew,
Arabic
Major Export: Polished
Diamonds
Major Import: Chemicals

Japan
Area: 145,869 sq mi
(377,801 sq km)
Population: 127,100,000
Capital: Tokyo
Language: Japanese
Major Export: Machinery
Major Import:
Manufactured Goods

Jordan
Area: 34,444 sq mi
(89,210 sq km)
Population: 5,200,000
Capital: Amman
Languages: Arabic
Major Export: Phosphates
Major Import: Crude Oil

Kazakhstan
Area: 1,049,039 sq mi
(2,716,998 sq km)
Population: 15,417,000
Capital: Astana
Languages: Kazakh,
Russian
Major Export: Petroleum
Major Import: Machinery

Korea, North
Area: 46,541 sq mi
(120,538 sq km)
Population: 22,000,000
Capital: Pyongyang
Language: Korean
Major Export: Minerals
Major Import: Petroleum

Korea, South
Area: 38,324 sq mi
(99,259 sq km)
Population: 48,800,000
Capital: Seoul
Language: Korean
Major Export: Electronic
Equipment
Major Import: Machinery

Kuwait
Area: 6,880 sq mi
(17,818 sq km)
Population: 2,300,000
Capital: Kuwait
Language: Arabic
Major Export: Petroleum
Major Import: Foods

Kyrgyzstan
Area: 76,641 sq mi
(198,500 sq km)
Population: 5,000,000
Capital: Bishkek
Languages: Kirghiz,
Russian (both official)
Major Export: Cotton
Major Import: Grain

Laos
Area: 91,429 sq mi
(236,800 sq km)
Population: 5,400,000
Capital: Vientiane
Languages: Lao, French
Major Export: Wood
Products
Major Import: Machinery

Lebanon
Area: 4,015 sq mi
(10,399 sq km)
Population: 4,300,000
Capital: Beirut
Languages: Arabic, French
Major Export: Paper
Major Import: Machinery

Malaysia
Area: 127,317 sq mi
(329,749 sq km)
Population: 22,700,000
Capital: Kuala Lumpur
Languages: Malay, English,
Chinese
Major Export: Electronic
Equipment
Major Import: Machinery

Maldives
Area: 116 sq mi
(300 sq km)
Population: 300,000
Capital: Male
Languages: Maldivian
Divehi, English
Major Export: Fish
Major Import: Machinery

Mongolia
Area: 604,826 sq mi
(1,566,499 sq km)
Population: 2,400,000
Capital: Ulaanbaatar
Language: Khalkha
Mongol
Major Export: Copper
Major Import: Fuels

Myanmar
Area: 261,228 sq mi
(676,581 sq km)
Population: 47,800,000
Capital: Yangon (Rangoon)
Languages: Burmese,
local languages
Major Export: Beans
Major Import: Machinery

Nepal
Area: 56,826 sq mi
(147,179 sq km)
Population: 23,500,000
Capital: Kathmandu
Language: Nepali
Major Export: Clothing
Major Import: Petroleum
Products

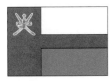

Oman
Area: 82,031 sq mi
(212,460 sq km)
Population: 2,400,000
Capital: Muscat
Language: Arabic
Major Export: Petroleum
Major Import: Machinery

Pakistan
Area: 307,375 sq mi
(796,101 sq km)
Population: 145,000,000
Capital: Islamabad
Languages: Urdu, English,
Punjabi, Sindhi
Major Export: Cotton
Major Import: Petroleum

Philippines
Area: 115,830 sq mi
(300,000 sq km)
Population: 77,200,000
Capital: Manila
Languages: Tagalog,
English (both official)
Major Export: Electronic
Equipment
Major Import:
Raw Materials

Qatar
Area: 4,247 sq mi
(11,000 sq km)
Population: 600,000
Capital: Doha
Language: Arabic
Major Export: Petroleum
Major Import: Machinery

Saudi Arabia
Area: 829,996 sq mi
(2,149,690 sq km)
Population: 21,100,000
Capital: Riyadh
Language: Arabic
Major Export: Petroleum
Major Import: Machinery

Singapore
Area: 239 sq mi
(619 sq km)
Population: 4,100,000
Capital: Singapore
Languages: Chinese,
Malay, Tamil, English
Major Export: Computer
Equipment
Major Import: Aircraft

Sri Lanka
Area: 25,332 sq mi
(65,610 sq km)
Population: 19,500,000
Capital: Colombo
Languages: Sinhalese,
Tamil, English
Major Export: Textiles
Major Import: Machinery

Syria
Area: 71,498 sq mi
(185,180 sq km)
Population: 17,100,000
Capital: Damascus
Languages: Arabic,
Kurdish, Armenian
Major Export: Petroleum
Major Import: Machinery

Tajikistan
Area: 55,251 sq mi
(143,100 sq km)
Population: 6,200,000
Capital: Dushanbe
Languages: Tajik, Russian
Major Export: Aluminum
Major Import: Fuels

Thailand
Area: 198,116 sq mi
(513,120 sq km)
Population: 62,400,000
Capital: Bangkok
Languages: Thai, local
languages
Major Export:
Manufactured Goods
Major Import: Machinery

Turkey
Area: 299,158 sq mi
(774,819 sq km)
Population: 66,300,000
Capital: Ankara
Languages: Turkish,
Kurdish
Major Export: Foods and
Livestock
Major Import: Machinery

Turkmenistan
Area: 188,456 sq mi
(488,101 sq km)
Population: 5,500,000
Capital: Ashgabat
Languages: Turkmen,
Russian, Uzbek
Major Export: Natural Gas
Major Import: Machinery

United Arab
Emirates
Area: 32,278 sq mi
(83,600 sq km)
Population: 3,300,000
Capital: Abu Dhabi
Languages: Arabic, Persian
Major Export: Petroleum
Major Import:
Manufactured Goods

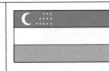

Uzbekistan
Area: 172,471 sq mi
(446,700 sq km)
Population: 25,100,000
Capital: Tashkent
Languages: Uzbek,
Russian, Tajik
Major Export: Cotton
Major Import: Machinery

Vietnam
Area: 128,066 sq mi
(331,691 sq km)
Population: 78,700,000
Capital: Hanoi
Languages: Vietnamese,
local languages
Major Export: Crude Oil
Major Import: Machinery

Yemen
Area: 203,849 sq mi
(527,969 sq km)
Population: 18,000,000
Capital: Sanaa
Language: Arabic
Major Export: Cotton
Major Import: Textiles

AUSTRALIA & OCEANIA

Australia
Area: 2,988,888 sq mi
(7,741,220 sq km)
Population: 19,400,000
Capital: Canberra
Language: English
Major Export: Coal
Major Import: Machinery

Fiji
Area: 7,054 sq mi
(18,270 sq km)
Population: 800,000
Capital: Suva
Languages: English, Fijian,
Hindi
Major Export: Sugar
Major Import: Machinery

Kiribati
Area: 282 sq mi
(730 sq km)
Population: 100,000
Capital: Tarawa
Languages: English,
Gilbertese
Major Export: Coconut
Products
Major Import: Foods

Marshall Islands
Area: 69 sq mi
(179 sq km)
Population: 100,000
Capital: Majuro
Languages: English, local
languages
Major Export: Coconut
Products
Major Import: Foods

Micronesia
Population: 270 sq mi
(699 sq km)
Population: 100,000
Capital: Palikir
Languages: English, local
languages
Major Export: Fish
Major Import: Foods

Nauru
Area: 9 sq mi
(23 sq km)
Population: 10,000
Capital: Yaren
Languages: Nauruan,
English
Major Export: Phosphates
Major Import: Foods

New Zealand
Area: 104,452 sq mi
(270,531 sq km)
Population: 3,900,000
Capital: Wellington
Language: English
Major Export: Wool
Major Import: Machinery

Palau
Area: 178 sq mi
(461 sq km)
Population: 20,000
Capital: Koror
Languages: English,
Palauan
Major Export: Fish
Major Import: Machinery

Papua New Guinea
Area: 178,703 sq mi
(462,841 sq km)
Population: 5,000,000
Capital: Port Moresby
Languages: English, local
languages
Major Export: Gold
Major Import: Machinery

Samoa
Area: 1,097 sq mi
(2,841 sq km)
Population: 200,000
Capital: Apia
Languages: Samoan,
English
Major Export: Coconut
Products
Major Import: Foods

Solomon Islands
Area: 11,158 sq mi
(28,899 sq km)
Population: 500,000
Capital: Honiara
Languages: English,
local languages
Major Export: Cocoa
Major Import: Machinery

Tonga
Area: 290 sq mi
(699 sq km)
Population: 100,000
Capital: Nuku'alofa
Languages: Tongan,
English
Major Export: Squash
Major Import: Foods

Tuvalu
Area: 10 sq mi
(26 sq km)
Population: 10,000
Capital: Funafuti
Languages: Tuvalu, English
Major Export: Coconut
Products
Major Import: Foods

Vanuatu
Area: 4,707 sq mi
(12,191 sq km)
Population: 200,000
Capital: Port-Vila
Languages: English,
French, Bislama
Major Export: Coconut
Products
Major Import: Machinery

World Facts & Figures

The Earth

AREA: 196,951,900 sq mi (510,066,000 sq km)

LAND: 57,313,000 sq mi (148,647,000 sq km)—29.1%

WATER: 139,638,900 sq mi (361,419,000 sq km)— 70.9%

POPULATION: 6,067,000,000 people

The Continents

	AREA (sq mi)	(sq km)	Percent of Earth's Land
Asia	17,213,300	44,579,000	30.0
Africa	11,609,000	30,065,000	20.2
North America	9,449,500	24,474,000	16.5
South America	6,880,500	17,819,000	12.0
Antarctica	5,100,400	13,209,000	8.9
Europe	3,837,400	9,938,000	6.7
Australia	2,968,200	7,687,000	5.2

Highest Point On Each Continent

	feet	meters
Everest, Asia	29,035	8,850
Aconcagua, South America	22,834	6,960
McKinley (Denali), N. America	20,320	6,194
Kilimanjaro, Africa	19,340	5,895
El'brus, Europe	18,510	5,642
Vinson Massif, Antarctica	16,067	4,897
Kosciuszko, Australia	7,310	2,228

Lowest Point On Each Continent

	feet	meters
Dead Sea, Asia	-1,349	-411
Lake Assal, Africa	-512	-156
Death Valley, N. America	-282	-86
Valdés Peninsula, S. America	-131	-40
Caspian Sea, Europe	-92	-28
Lake Eyre, Australia	-52	-16
Antarctica (ice covered)	-8,366	-2,550

Ten Longest Rivers

	LENGTH miles	kilometers
Nile, Africa	4,241	6,825
Amazon, South America	4,000	6,437
Yangtze (Chang), Asia	3,964	6,380
Mississippi-Missouri, N. America	3,710	5,971
Yenisey-Angara, Asia	3,440	5,536
Yellow (Huang), Asia	3,395	5,464
Ob-Irtysh, Asia	3,361	5,410
Amur, Asia	2,744	4,416
Lena, Asia	2,734	4,400
Congo, Africa	2,715	4,370

Ten Largest Lakes

	AREA (Sq mi)	(Sq km)	Greatest Depth (feet)	(meters)
Caspian Sea, Europe-Asia	143,254	371,000	3,363	1,025
Superior, N. America	31,701	82,100	1,332	406
Victoria, Africa	26,836	69,500	269	82
Huron, N. America	23,013	59,600	751	229
Michigan, N. America	22,318	57,800	922	281
Tanganyika, Africa	12,587	32,600	4,823	1,470
Baikal, Asia	12,163	31,500	5,371	1,637
Great Bear, N. America	12,086	31,300	1,463	446
Aral Sea, Asia	11,854	30,700	167	51
Malawi, Africa	11,159	28,900	2,280	695

Ten Largest Islands

	AREA (Sq mi)	(Sq km)
Greenland	840,065	2,175,600
New Guinea	306,008	792,500
Borneo	280,137	725,500
Madagascar	226,658	587,000
Baffin	195,961	507,500
Sumatra	164,993	427,300
Honshu	87,806	227,400
Great Britain	84,215	218,100
Victoria	83,906	217,300
Ellesmere	75,759	196,200

The Oceans

	AREA (Sq mi)	(Sq km)	Percent of Earth's Water Area
Pacific	64,190,671	166,241,000	46.0
Atlantic	33,422,271	86,557,000	23.9
Indian	28,352,382	73,427,000	20.3
Arctic	3,662,445	9,485,000	2.6

Deepest Point In Each Ocean

	feet	meters
Challenger Deep, Mariana Trench, Pacific	35,827	10,920
Puerto Rico Trench, Atlantic	28,232	8,605
Java Trench, Indian	23,376	7,125
Molloy Deep, Arctic	18,399	5,608

Ten Largest Seas

	AREA (Sq mi)	(Sq km)	Average Depth (feet)	(meters)
South China	1,148,583	2,974,600	4,803	1,464
Caribbean	971,465	2,515,900	8,448	2,575
Mediterranean	969,187	2,510,000	4,924	1,501
Bering	873,079	2,261,100	4,892	1,491
Gulf of Mexico	582,130	1,507,600	5,298	1,615
Sea of Okhotsk	537,532	1,392,100	3,192	973
Sea of Japan	391,111	1,012,900	5,469	1,667
Hudson Bay	281,912	730,100	305	93
East China	256,622	664,600	620	189
Andaman	218,125	564,900	3,668	1,118

Earth's Extremes

HOTTEST PLACE: Dalol, Denakil Depression, Ethiopia; annual average temperature— 93°F (34°C)

COLDEST PLACE: Plateau Station, Antarctica; annual average temperature— -134°F (-56.7°C)

WETTEST PLACE: Mawsynram, Assam, India; annual average rainfall— 467 in (1,187.3 cm)

DRIEST PLACE: Atacama Desert, Chile; rainfall barely measurable

HIGHEST WATERFALL: Angel, Venezuela— 3,212ft (979 m)

LARGEST DESERT: Sahara, Africa— 3,475,000 sq mi (9,000,000 sq km)

LARGEST CANYON: Grand Canyon, Colorado River, Arizona; 277 mi (446 km) long along river; 1,801 ft (549 m) to 18 mi (29 km) wide, about 1 mi (1.6 km) deep

LONGEST REEF: Great Barrier Reef, Australia— 1,250 mi (2,012 km)

GREATEST TIDES: Bay of Fundy, Nova Scotia— 52 ft (16 m)